The Simple Gift of Joy

Ali Todd

ISBN- 9798511025087

Cover design by: The Butterfly Creation

Printed in the United Kingdom

This book is dedicated to my lockdown heroes - my Mum, my son Ryan, my friend Fi, the lady over the road and every other brave person who survived lockdown whilst living alone.

Contents

4

Introduction

How to use this book to HELP others.

If all goes to plan then you are about to read a book that was written by a friend of a friend of a friend. (That's me) Here's how you can help: I am raising money for the mental health charity MIND. For every single sale (e-book or paperback) I make, one pound will be donated. My mammoth goal is one million pounds! A very clever lady recently showed me that it only takes twenty steps to hit this target. Seriously - just twenty!

So, if I give this book to just one friend, this could happen: They buy a copy of the book for at least two loved ones. Then every person who ever gets given this wonderful gift duplicates the same act of kindness. So all I ask is that you buy a copy of this book for two people you care about. Visit my website to buy the eBook or paperback
https://thesimplegiftofjoy.com

You can find instructions on how to buy a Kindle book as a gift on my website or at Amazon (My preference as I am a bit of a green freak)

STEPS

1) I give one book for free and that person buys two copies for their nearest and dearest, raising:

2) £2 for MIND   then step   3) £4 for MIND

4) £8   5) £16

and so on........

6) £32   7) £64   8) £128

9) £256   10) £512   11) £1,024

12) £2,048   13) £4,096   14) £8,192

15) £16,384   16) £32,768   17) £65,536

18) £131,072   19) £262,144   20) £524,288

Add all the above amounts to this whopping sum at step 20 and there you have your million plus raised for a brilliant cause!

Best of all, though, I hope this book helps a million people to capture their own little moments of JOY!!

How to use this book to help yourself.

Try to do at least one of the things every day. Some of the suggestions are intended to become daily habits, and some are just occasional boosts - small things to create a bigger, more joyful picture. I have tried to list, at the back, every self-help book I have ever read that may have contributed to the advice I lay out here. I also mention any websites that may be of interest. I definitely quote some of the wise people I know and love too and will try to give credit where it's due.

DISCLAIMER: This book comes straight from my heart with the loving intention of helping people to find joy. If you are suffering from severe depression, anxiety or any other serious mental illness then definitely use the ideas in the book to help you. At the same time, I urge you to seek professional help.

Prologue

I was inspired to write this book by a story of loneliness. My friend has a son who has Autism. I was his teacher once, many years ago. He was an adorable child and is now a very exceptional young man. One day there was a call from his college saying that he was wandering around the place during lockdown 'trying to talk to people' and that it 'had to stop.'

He was simply seeking human connection - the most fundamental of human joys. He was not even a person who lived alone. The story broke my heart and made me angry all at the same time.

I had heard other such stories - an elderly gentleman being reported to the police for making dog walkers feel uncomfortable - he too, it transpired, just wanted a chat, contact with others - something we are hard wired for in order to survive and thrive.

So this book came to me. It's not a solution to all the woes of the world, by any means; I can't cure or stop the spread of viruses, I can't make our governments serve the people better and I can't put an end to loneliness or hunger. What I hope I can do is help - just a little bit - by pointing you towards joyful ways of being.

The recipe for this book is drawn from a lifetime addiction to self-help books, trainings and therapies and is as follows: - a hefty dollop of science; a dash of common sense; a large pinch of intuition; a generous sprinkling of authenticity; an extravagant helping of love; a long, slow bake in the oven of experience and a fancy topping of hope. I have spent hundreds, if not thousands of hours (and pounds) reading loads of self-help books so you don't have to.

PART ONE - WORK

Definitions

work: to be effective or successful

work: physical or mental effort to accomplish something.

work: to shape, change or process

Chapter 1

Do a good deed

"No act of kindness, no matter how small, is ever wasted.' - Aesop."

A good deed equals shared joy. Try to do a good deed every day. No matter how small, doing good is guaranteed to make you feel amazing. It's one of our most basic human traits - we are hardwired to help others. We are primed to be tribal, to work together, to help each other because early on in man's evolution, belonging to a tribe, strength in numbers, was the key to survival. So connection, belonging and collaboration as well as acts of kindness are all inherent in us.

A great example I saw of this was during my experience as a teacher in the playground. Despite being told by a very eminent psychiatrist that kids under six are, by definition, psychopaths (these days we say 'sociopath' to distinguish from the serial killer variety,) I witnessed, on countless occasions, beautiful acts of loving kindness that completely busted the myth that 'kids are cruel.' A child would fall over and invariably another would rush over to help them up and check they were ok. It was heart-warming to see.

So, if you want to feel joy, go out there and do something for another person for no other reason than to help or make another human feel good. Acts of altruism make the giver feel just as good. The 'helper's high' is fuelled by oxytocin - the bonding hormone that is released in the brain, so maybe selfless acts are selfish after all. But that still doesn't explain why someone would dive into freezing water, risking their own life, to save that of a stranger.

Ultimately, who cares whether you are really doing it to feel good or to help someone else feel good? It's a brilliant double whammy with an added side effect of helping with loneliness. I can't really think of a scenario where doing a good deed made anyone feel bad (despite the saying 'no good deed goes unpunished') unless the motive is not genuine. If you are trying to assuage your own feelings of guilt about something then you probably won't get the same happy vibe as if you were honestly just doing something out of the goodness of your heart.

So don't call or visit Granny because you feel bad that it's been so long, or you're worried about the will; do it because you genuinely want to see her. Don't reluctantly hand in that wallet full of cash you found but do it willingly because you can imagine yourself in the hapless owner's shoes and really want to get it back to them. Give blood, offer to help someone struggling with too many bags, bring your neighbour's empty bins in when you know they are at work, use your imagination to come up with small ways you can help others.

Chapter 2

Plant and grow something.

"Gardening is cheaper than therapy – and you get tomatoes." —
Anonymous

Plant, grow or care for something living - talk to it, nurture it, care whether it lives or dies. You don't have to be Prince Charles to do this one and a house plant is as beneficial as a full-blown garden. Science has proven that caring for a plant - the simple act of being responsible for a living entity, gives us a purpose in life, even if it's a tiny one. This is particularly important as we get older when we no longer have others to care for.

Studies in care homes have found that people are more motivated when they have the simple task of caring for a live plant - it adds purpose to their life and provides the brain with the rewards associated with joy. Growing something from scratch can be wholly satisfying too. It's a wonderful feeling to see the tiniest green shoot emerge when you have planted seeds or bulbs. All the waiting fades into oblivion and it's easy to feel as though it was you, not the miraculous life force of Mother Nature, that made it happen.

In addition to the benefits of being in charge of a living being's survival (or not), there are physical gains to be had from having live plants in your house. They are perfect for clearing the air, cleansing our environment and making the place look nice. We are naturally drawn towards areas of greenery, because it stimulates a part of the brain that causes us to become calm.

Anyone who is familiar with small children will know that they seldom need persuading to go outside. The main reason for this is that fresh air feels good and it also feels great to run around in open spaces. It seems the greenery part of nature is a big factor too. Studies have shown that green areas can help improve their learning capacity and behaviour when compared to play that takes place in a normal concrete school yard with no natural surrounds.

Even for adults, just the colour green has a powerful effect on the psyche. In office spaces with greenery, even when the plants are artificial, lower stress levels are reported by the employees compared to environments where there is no greenery of any kind. I am not recommending fake house plants, although they could offer the benefit of the 'green effect.' But imagine the joy when you actually helped that real, living, breathing greenery to thrive!

Chapter 3

Learn a new skill

"Learning a new skill can change hundreds of millions of cortical connections."- Michael Merzenich

Why learn a new skill? Well, this book is all about JOY, right? Having novel, stimulating experiences releases dopamine in the brain. We like dopamine.

In addition, breaking with mundane routine can make time appear to expand; have you ever noticed how quickly the days, months, years speed by when you are doing the same old, same old? Living on autopilot?

For me personally, the year of Covid saw me in the most boring rut of a routine I have ever had. I am not saying that routine is bad; it definitely has its place - an important role to play in some areas of our lives. It's just that the days can blur into one. However, I am a bit of a stimulus junkie - I love trying new things and I particularly love learning.

'Changing it up' also has a markedly positive effect on the ageing of your brain. We talk about 'sitting there, rotting.' That is certainly what it feels like when there is nothing new in life. Contrary to what science used to believe, it's now known that your brain can regenerate as it forms new neural pathways.

It gives me great joy and motivation to know that my intuition was right: learning new things is good for us. Some brilliant skills for activating diverse areas of the brain are: dancing; learning a new language, or how to play a musical instrument; painting; in fact anything creative and I will go into this in more detail later.

A good place to start is to mirror someone else who has already mastered whatever it is you want to learn. If you want to get really good at something more quickly, you could even try the Raikov method.

Raikov was a Russian scientist who conducted research into mind-set, hypnosis and mastering new skills. He gave the subjects of his study a post-hypnotic suggestion that enabled them to 'channel' a famous person already successful in their chosen area, such as music.

He discovered that it was possible for these human guinea pigs to master things to a much higher level by believing they were well known geniuses.

Learning a new skill seems to get more difficult as you get older. I always used to pride myself on being a quick learner. Disappointingly, my brain is not as quick as it used to be and I have to work harder at mastering new things.

Yet, I would never allow this fact to stop me trying and this is where using the Raikov method helps.

So imagine if you want to get better at painting, for example, you might put yourself into the mind of Vincent Van Gogh or Rembrandt. You might want to channel Brian May if you are learning the guitar.

I am not saying that only high level, fame-inducing talent is worth aspiring to. Any new thing you try to get to grips with is a great stimulation to the joy-inducing stuff in our brain.

Maybe you want to learn something as basic as how to crochet a blanket, in which case you could buy an instruction book or find an online tutorial. But there is nothing to stop you from channelling your granny who is a master of the crochet hook!

Chapter 4

Be part of a community or tribe

"Alone, we can do so little; together, we can do so much" – Helen Keller

Human beings are pre-programmed to crave a feeling of belonging. It was crucial to our survival in prehistoric times because rejection from our tribe meant almost-certain death.

Even today, it's one of the most powerful drives we have. To be accepted, respected, and liked is to be human. And it goes beyond this. Being part of any kind of community, tribe or team can be greatly rewarding and joyful.

It doesn't matter whether you belong to a sports team, a political group, a choir, a hobby or interest club or even just a group of friends or family. The benefits are universal and simple: sharing, influencing, connecting, learning, growing, supporting and reinforcing.

Sharing ideas and experiences is a great way to expand and grow. In a team sport you may learn techniques from team mates. In a friendship group you may have role models, whilst not realising that you are exactly that role model to someone else.

Even in something as simple as a social media group you may get the support and understanding you have not found elsewhere. (I am still an old-fashioned advocate of real life human interactions and believe that being in each other's physical presence helps us to share that crucial, invisible energy that we hippies call the 'aura.')

Shared identity is hugely important for mental health and the feel good factor because, ironically, we all naturally tend to feel 'different' when in fact, even in this belief alone, we are alike.

It's a great feeling to come to the realisation that others feel as we do, suffer as we do, live and love in just the same way as we do.

Community allows us to share our strengths and weaknesses, to reinforce our positive traits and have them appreciated by others. Give and take. It's the stuff of life.

Being part of a group is particularly beneficial for loners like me - despite my outward confidence I am shy and am definitely not a natural at forging friendships.

I love my book group in that respect. There is nothing I enjoy more than making them laugh and I always come away feeling like I belong, like I have learned something, knowing that I aspire to be a little more like so-and-so (each one of them, in fact), that I have both added value to the experience and taken away great lessons, ideas, feelings and hopes.

Every small tribe I belong to gives me joy, from my small group of girlfriends from secondary school to a Facebook group I'm a member of with twenty thousand struggling teachers, every one of which seems to have lived my exact experience!

Chapter 5

Exercise

"Exercise is a celebration of what your body can do. Not a punishment for what you ate." Anonymous

For some of us, the words 'exercise' and 'joy' do not necessarily belong in the same sentence. That is simply because we have not yet found the right exercise for us. In order to change that, it's useful to evaluate what exercise means. In its simplest definition, it just means to move your body in addition to the essential moving it does to live your everyday life.

One indisputable fact about exercise on a scientific level is that it releases hormones called endorphins and other feel good hormones. There is a lot of complicated science behind why exercise makes you feel good but essentially, it equates to 'exercise can be a brilliant source of joy.'

So, if you are a natural gym-bunny then I don't need to persuade you that exercising is not only good for your physical health but it also feels good and has great mental health benefits. If, like me, you are not a natural, then have a think about what sort of physical activity you actually enjoy. A good place to start is walking. It's something that most of us can do. The beauty is that it can be incorporated into normal life, it involves no cost and it's as easy or as hard as you want to make it.

Dancing is another great, joyful way to exercise and has enough benefits to merit its own chapter in this book. (Chapter 55)

Something that I think is vital when it comes to maintaining a regular exercise regime is to change it up. Boredom with the same old thing is something that often gets in my way when it comes to being a successful, regular exerciser and if that sounds like you then I recommend doing something different as often as possible.

As a deep thinker, someone who could happily sit at desk writing and exploring ideas for hours on end, I have to remind myself every day that I need to get out of my head and back into my body. I need to remember that I am human and not just a disconnected brain. I need to remind myself that it feels good celebrating what my body can do, pushing it to do something a tiny bit better than it could yesterday.

Something that has come to light in recent studies is that it's not enough to just do your three or five workouts per week if you are in a sedentary job. It's almost equally important to get up regularly and move in some way or another throughout your day. I have recently started taking five minute breaks with a hula hoop or skipping rope but it could just as well be star jumps, jogging on the spot or press ups.

Here are just a few ideas: walk, run, cycle, dance, roller skate, climb, swim, row, ski, water ski, surf, golf, tennis, team sports, yoga, Pilates, ballet, the list is endless. One thing that is essential is to try to incorporate some aerobic, some stretching and plenty of strength work. High Intensity Interval Training (HIIT) has become popular recently and with good reason - you do a good, hard, quick workout and it's done - perfect for these busy times!

Just a quick note on strength - sadly there does not seem to be enough publicity aimed at 'women of a certain age' and the crucial role of strength training in keeping strong healthy bones and muscles. I did a little research after my mum had her second fractured vertebrae (with no apparent cause) because I wanted to avoid having to suffer as she does. It's crucial to do some form of weight bearing exercise and also some weight lifting and resistance work. Having your body pack up on you is definitely not conducive to joy.

Chapter 6

Create a morning ritual

"Lose an hour in the morning, and you will spend all day looking for it." - *Richard Whately*

Start a morning ritual. Yes, I know this appears to be a direct contradiction to my previous words of wisdom about breaking the monotony but, as I said, there is a time and a place.

To start the day, there is nothing better than having a clear routine, to kick off the day in a positive way. Plenty of famous, successful, happy people advocate it.

Even if you're not a morning person, just give it a try for a few days and if you can stretch it out for twenty one to twenty eight days then it will begin to embed as a new habit.

Getting up ahead of the rest of the world is a wonderful feeling. Nothing quite beats an hour of peace and quiet before the day begins to come alive. The time is all yours to use as you wish and I recommend using it wisely if you want to feel great for the rest of the day.

Most importantly, use it for yourself. It could be that you simply meditate for five minutes or write affirmations while you wait for your coffee to brew. If sitting, pondering on the loo for twenty minutes is your thing then who am I to judge? Or maybe you like to get your daily exercise out of the way. Yoga is a fabulous way to start the day but sometimes just a good stretch feels great too - my dog, Buzz seems to know this instinctively.

My absolute favourite 'first thing in the morning' act is borrowed from a lovely friend of mine. Every morning before she does a single thing, she sits up in bed and smiles for a full sixty seconds. What a great way to start the day! I'm still working on forming it as a habit and I do forget sometimes but the intention is there.

You may want to make it more formal - try the Miracle Morning ritual outlined by the remarkable Hal Elrod with his six 'life savers.'

You are definitely the best judge of what will work for you, though, and one person's ideal could be another's cringe. For example one of the things Hal advises is saying positive affirmations. I love the idea of this but putting it into practice is just too embarrassing for me to do out loud, even in front of my most intimate loved ones, so I try to do these out loud in the car on the way to work (in between bouts of singing at the top of my lungs).

If you can perfect the art of getting out of bed on the right side then you will reap some wonderful rewards. They include: better self-organisation and clarity; less forgetfulness; increased productivity and creativity; a more positive mind-set and a fully energised mind, body and soul. In other words: increased levels of joy.

Even if you simply make a habit of telling yourself you are enough, or you make a heartfelt wish for world peace before you start each day, you will feel joy.

I sincerely believe in a collective human consciousness and therefore the more people focusing on the idea of a clean, fair, peaceful and happy world must surely have an impact eventually?

Beware of making your morning routine so cast-in-stone that it becomes a rut - my mantra is 'rules are made to be broken' and you will see the common theme throughout this book that variety is also a good thing for stimulating drive and creativity.

Chapter 7

Tidy up

"The best way to find out what we really need is to get rid of what we don't." - Marie Kondō."

Tidy up. Declutter. My mum always used to say 'tidy house, tidy mind' and I would roll my eyes. As with many of her pearls of wisdom, I have now realised she was right all along.

I tend to put off the act of tidying and cleaning or any other job that I perceive will just need doing all over again. Just ask my kids how I would practically expect them to levitate above floor level rather than walk on any cleaning I had just accomplished - woe betide anyone who dared to undo my efforts!

So yes, I do like my living space to be clean and tidy. And I know that lots of people love cleaning. They find it soothing, meditative. When I actually force myself to get stuck in, it soon becomes apparent that there is something satisfying about completing domestic chores and that it's all about being in the moment. If you worry about the inevitable fact of your hard work being undone then you can be guaranteed disappointment. The key is enjoying the process, the journey because the 'now' of reaching 'destination tidy' is inevitably short-lived in any busy household.

On an energetic level, having a clean and tidy home is the first step towards ensuring that your root chakra is balanced and healthy. Another word for this chakra is the base. It's the foundation of the building that is our metaphorical 'house,' the symbolic roots of our own tree of life. And for this reason I love the title of the Marie Kondo book The Life Changing Magic of Tidying. (I must get round to reading it someday.)

An emphasis on decluttering is probably more satisfying and less short lived than cleaning and, as a bit of a hoarder, I love the idea of 'if you don't love it, then ditch it.'

Disclaimer - those of you who know me will laugh and know that this part of practicing what I preach is very much at the 'work in progress' stage!

Chapter 8

Daydream

"Everything starts as somebody's daydream." - Larry Niven."

Daydream. Fantasise. I definitely practise this part of my preaching! For me, it's about having hope. Use your imagination to picture what you would love your life to look like. Be unrestricted with this activity. Be brave. Bold. Refuse to be held back by the bounds of 'realistic.' Embody the expression 'in your wildest dreams.' Don't just think about it with your brain, feel it in your heart. Really get into it and experience the feelings you would feel if this was actually the life you were living. Feel JOY, excitement, elation, contentment, love.

Not everyone believes in the Law of Attraction but its many proponents swear that the use of emotion is the most crucial part of manifesting the life you deserve. Of all the positive emotions you can think of, gratitude is the gold standard.

If you want to take it beyond just escapist fantasy then be sure to include plenty of detail. What colour is that car you want? What about the interior? Is it leather or cloth? What size is the engine? Is it hybrid? Fully electric? How does it feel to drive it?

Just have fun with it. Play with it. Use it as a fun activity to take yourself into a different realm and whatever you do, do NOT fall into the trap of letting it make you focus on all the things your life isn't. There is nothing to be gained from that.

Creating a vision board is great as a tool to manifest your dreams. My own preferred method of successfully achieving goals is to first write them down (I'm more driven by words than pictures), then break them into steps and then do my best to take action towards them.

REALITY CHECK. Unfortunately, you have to take action if there is something you truly desire in life. I wish it were otherwise but, sadly, you cannot just lie in a bed and expect the magic to shimmy up the drainpipe and tap on the window pane into your world (believe me - I've tried it) and who would have it any other way? It's much more fun going out into that big wide world and getting it.

I love going back to my wish lists and surprising myself, later on, at just how many of the goals I have actually met. My most wonderful manifestation to date is my life partner whose 'spec' I wrote down in the notes section of my iPhone on a new moon (yes, I know it's a bit 'woo woo' but that's me) precisely TWO days before we met at a school reunion that I didn't even know I was going to, thirty years after we had last seen each other!

Another useful tip if you want to create a vision board is to first of all meditate on what you desire - slipping into a relaxed state of alpha brainwaves is a very powerful way of tapping in to your heart's desire rather than just thinking you should want the latest trendy car that everyone else has. It can also be helpful to divide your list or your mind map or collage into what you want to BE, DO and HAVE in your life because it's definitely not all about dreaming up material possessions.

Chapter 9

Make a new friend

"The great thing about new friends is that they bring new energy to your soul." – Shanna Rodriguez

Make a new friend. I did this recently and I'm usually rubbish at making new friends. With social media nowadays, it's easier to reach out to someone you don't really know. It could be someone you've only met once or twice but clicked with or have lots in common with. Tune in to your intuition to gauge the energy they carry into your field - if you get positive vibes then you are probably going to add value in some way to each other's lives.

Next time you or another person says 'we must get together,' instead of just letting it slide and never happen, make it happen. I guarantee it will be worth it. People come into our lives for a definite reason, just as they sometimes leave our lives too. Perhaps we need different friends for different stages in our life. What we get from our work friendships could be different than a fellow parent from the playground or an old school buddy that you always got on well with.

Take the initiative and reach out. You have nothing to lose and everything to gain. For some reason children find this much easier to do than adults do. So be like a child, just make the first move and tell someone you like their shoes or their hair or ask them out for coffee because inviting them out to play may sound a bit weird!

Chapter 10

Spend time with old friends

"New friends may be poems but old friends are alphabets. Don't forget the alphabets because you will need them to read the poems." - William Shakespeare

Make time for your old friends. There is something uniquely special about friends who have known you for donkey's years. They know the real you. They usually know you warts and all, inside out and upside down. And, whilst this may not sit comfortably with anyone who has added new layers of pretension to their outer persona (and let's face it, most of us adopt some airs into adulthood to mask and hide the 'self' we secretly believe to be not good enough) it can be refreshingly liberating to be around people who know our ridiculous middle name, who can remember our teeth before braces or the hairstyle we innocently turned up with at Uni (mine was a horrid, home-dyed yellow perm.)

My oldest friends are still the ones I feel that I really can be myself around. My theory is that we are bound by fun and laughter; ultimately we are bound by joy: the joy of youth. Next time you spot a close-knit group of people between the ages of five and twenty-five, just watch how much they laugh. Of course nowadays you may have to wait for a while 'til they all get off their phones!

The one thing that is important to remember when it comes to friends is that it's a two way transaction. The beauty of having friends is that you can choose them. There is no law that says you have to stick with an energy vampire who puts you down just because your mothers were friends and you've been forced together since the age of three. If you have 'frenemies' who make you feel bad then trade them in.

When you come away from spending time with friends you should feel enriched, inspired, uplifted and confident that you have given the same energy in return. Of course friends are there to go through the thick and thin and we all need a shoulder to cry on. I am not saying life and friendship is always a bed of roses - just that friendship needs to be a balance of give and take in order for it to be a joyful experience.

Chapter 11

Keep a journal

"Journaling is like whispering to one's self and listening at the same time." Mina Murray

There is a very good reason why I say keep rather than start a journal. As with much of my advice, it's about forming habits. Journaling is the go-to recommendation of pretty much every self-development 'guru' out there, and they are right. I have started so many journals I lose count. But rather than beating myself up about forgetting or falling out of the habit, I simply start again, safe in the knowledge that a habit can easily be formed in just 21 days or so of repeated action.

What type of journal you write is up to you. Many people opt for a gratitude journal. This is one of the easiest to start with and there are loads of lovely journals you can buy with prompts - including my own. (Shameless plug - apologies.)

On the other hand, you may decide to opt for a twofold journal and I quite like this idea. You simply write all your positive thoughts at the front, and all your negative ones at the back. You may even choose to have two journals, especially if you believe that the negative, venting aspect of your 'back end' journal could contaminate the positive, optimistic writing in the front.

The benefit of venting onto paper is that it purges the nasty stuff. It's a brilliant tool for getting rid of anger at yourself or someone else because you can get it all off your chest without the pain of confrontation (I'm not suggesting you avoid important issues in this way).

If you want to take it a step further and really get rid of all the bad stuff then I recommend, when you're ready to let go, that you burn the pages in order to completely release all that negative energy.

In her brilliant book, The Artist's Way, Julia Cameron promotes the writing of three pages each day as soon as you wake up. You literally write non-stop, the first things that come into your mind.

If you are not keen on the idea of spilling your soul onto a page, then why not do what my dad has done all his life and just write a record of the day? This could be as simple as what you did, what the weather was like and other small details, and then you could graduate onto including the occasional feeling, mood or emotion. It certainly does not have to be a daily, in-depth study of your every innermost thought in order to be beneficial.

Whichever type of journaling turns out to suit you best, just try to stick with it for a while. I can guarantee it will help you clarify your joy and learn a bit more about yourself.

Chapter 12

Quit a bad habit

"Saying NO to the wrong things creates space to say YES to the right things." – Mack Story

Quitting a bad habit - even a really small one - will lead to a huge sense of accomplishment and can be brilliant for joy-filled self-esteem. Crushing a bad habit does not have to mean giving up a lifelong twenty cigarettes a day addiction, although that would be great.

You could simply be trying really hard not to bite your nails, or to stop calling yourself an idiot every time you mess up.

It could be as simple as putting the rubbish out the night before collection instead of rushing out of the house in your pyjamas the minute you hear the lorry pull into your road.

If you really want to give up a destructive habit like smoking, drugs or alcohol then I highly recommend having an RTT (Rapid Transformational Therapy) session with a qualified practitioner like myself. (Another shameless plug!)

Some useful tips to help you on your journey:

Tell people your plans - having accountability increases your level of commitment.

Have a clear focus on your 'why' to help you maintain momentum - if you have a good reason to give up something destructive then that reason is not likely to just vanish overnight.

Remove temptation - why make things harder on yourself? I remember years ago giving up smoking whilst keeping an open pack in the house just to prove to myself how very 'over it' I was. Needless to say, it was not the last time I quit.

Try to replace the old habit with a new good one. Be careful with this one - the new habit must be something that won't harm you otherwise it defeats the object. Having a glass of water every time you crave a smoke could be really helpful, but chewing gum or sucking sweets maybe less so.

Break the journey down into smaller, easier chunks. Baby steps are good and tomorrow never comes. If you tell yourself 'I will not drink alcohol this week' then there is no reason why you cannot just keep going and marking off the weeks - whereas 'forever' sometimes feels too daunting.

Be proud of your achievements. Celebrate and congratulate yourself on every success and beware of 'nay' sayers. In other words, take care to surround yourself with people who will support you and avoid the smoking or drinking buddy who feels threatened that you might be ditching not only your addiction but them too! The same goes for the friend who preferred it when you were both fat together.

I am proud of being a non-smoker and alcohol free but I do still remember how annoying it could be to hear the evangelical self-praise of reformed smokers, drinkers, sugar fiends, chocoholics, overeaters and all-round defeaters of anything else 'bad.' Particularly when I was nowhere close to consider quitting myself.

I suppose, like many people with addictive tendencies, my own biggest personal challenge is to overcome the mysterious 'gap' I've spent most of my life trying to fill with either food, booze, sugar or various things you can smoke. This void or emptiness that so many suffer from usually boils down quite simply to feeling 'not good enough,' or not feeling whole or complete in some way.

I can only hope that in quitting some of these destructive habits, I am closer to mastering the art of loving myself.

Chapter 13

Rekindle your passions

"I would rather die of passion than of boredom." – Vincent Van Gogh

Have a passion. If you don't feel you have one yet, it's never too late to try to find one. It helps to be clear on what it means to have a passion. Here are some things that probably don't count as a passion:

Your kids - we all love our kids. But we also all need something that is just for us. I'm talking about something outside of day to day family life that lights your fire and is your thing.

Cooking - same thing. We all have to eat and just because you enjoy preparing the family meal, does not make it a passion. Cooking is a passion when you do it for the sake of it; when you bake, create your own recipes, dream of going on Master Chef or Bake-Off or you simply love it so much you want to make it your business or job.

Your religion. You may feel passionate about your faith but I believe a passion is something that you do. An action that you take.

You get the idea, hopefully.

Here are a few things that I believe could count as a passion.

Books - reading them, even writing them or possibly collecting them.

Music - going to see live music, collecting records, playing or writing music, making playlists. Finding out about new music scenes/bands.

Sport - here the list is endless and in order to count as a passion it definitely needs to be more than just liking watching all sport on TV.

Art - creating it, appreciating it, buying it, and going to see it exhibited.

Travel - not just going on holiday once or twice a year or saying 'I would love to go to.....' but travel that becomes one of your life missions. If you always have a bucket list of places and sights you plan to visit then that is probably a passion.

Hobbies - Hiking, Knitting, Caving, Climbing, Photography, A Specific Sport. I would class a hobby as something you spend time doing on a weekly basis. For me the purpose of a hobby is to help me get out of my head (meaning a distraction from thinking not recreational drug use!)

It should be something that takes you away from the humdrum and helps you to switch off.

It makes you forget your worries. You look forward to doing this activity. It makes you feel good. It makes you happy, even if that only lasts while you are engaged in it.

Chapter 14

Find your purpose

"Your purpose is hidden within your wounds." - Rune Lazuli

Having a passion in life should not be confused with having a purpose. Passions come and go - they are emotionally driven and usually relate to something you love doing - something you are really 'into.'

Whereas your purpose in life is more focused and is usually driven by serving others or achieving something deeper - a more long lasting legacy.

The two things may or may not be linked. So you could have a passion for photography but your purpose is to promote awareness of global warming through your photojournalism in the Arctic.

On the other hand, your passion and your purpose may not be linked at all. You may be passionate about collecting Victorian antiques but know that your purpose in life is to nurse patients in palliative end-of-life care.

Being the butterfly that I am, my passions change on a weekly basis - in lockdown it was baking cakes. My latest is learning the steel tongue drum (I'm still learning Twinkle Twinkle.) Yet my purpose remains consistent.

My purpose is to help lead others to emotional and physical healing and feel great about themselves. In short, it's to help people find their joy. Funny that.

Chapter 15

Be a good news person

"The good news is that Jesus is coming back. The bad news is that he's really pissed off." - Bob Hope.

Try to be a good news person. As an empath, I really struggle with watching the news with all its depressing harbingers of doom and gloom.

Yet, I feel a little irresponsible if I just bury my head in the sand and ignore it completely. Instead, whenever possible I try to spin the news on its head. So for example, when Covid cases and deaths were being reported, I sent out a genuine prayer to all those affected and then I would try to calculate the number of survivors there must now be.

When the weather report says rain, I simply give thanks that the plants and beautiful greenery of my lovely country will be watered. I always equate snow with fun rather than inconvenience. Some of us are more naturally predisposed towards positivity than others but it's definitely a skill that can be learned and improved upon. Practice definitely makes perfect in this instance.

One of the main things you can do to raise your vibration into a more joy-filled place is to pay attention to what you choose to watch on TV. I realised during lockdown that we were watching loads of crime thrillers and that meant a lot of my vibrational space was being filled with serial killers and violence.

It does not sit comfortably with me because I soak it up too easily. It's the main reason I stopped writing a thriller a few years ago - I realised I want to be sending happy and positive energy out into the world. Of course I am not naive enough to think the world can always be hearts and flowers and besides, my intellect loves a good mystery.

You will see in chapter 22 that I fully endorse recognising our shadow side - everything in the world is balance. Sometimes, though, we need to take a step backwards to actually see where the scales are tipping.

Chapter 16

Write your own eulogy

"No one is actually dead until the ripples they cause in the world die away." Terry Pratchett

What has death got to do with joy? Well, this bit is actually more about living than dying. What is your legacy? What have you contributed to the world? All too many of us struggle with answering that question because we believe ourselves too insignificant. It's never too late to make a difference but if you don't think you have already made any kind of mark on the world then I can tell you, categorically, that you are wrong.

I do not need to know the first thing about you to know this. Every human on the planet has added something to the melting pot of mankind - no matter how small and humble.

Have you ever made another person laugh, think, or even cry? Have you ever given someone something they have been grateful for? Or done something kind for anyone? If you have any happy memories then they are undoubtedly shared with others. All those things are marks you made on the world.

Now, all you need to do is think a bit more consciously about how you want the rest of the marks you make to look. If you are still alive and reading this book then there is still time to add great things to your eulogy, starting from today.

Cliché alert! Guess what? Today is the first day of the rest of your life.

How do you want your life to look in a year? What will you have achieved? What might you have contributed to the world? Who and what will you be surrounded by in the future? What kind of person will you be?

We cannot aim for anything if we don't know exactly what it is we want. Once you are clear, all you have to do is set yourself on a path - take the first step.

What song will sum up your life? What will others say about you? Be honest about this bit. Often, other people like us a lot more than we like ourselves, a lot more than we realise. It's not a sin but a virtue to think highly of yourself.

Chapter 17

Set yourself a challenge

"One of the secrets of life is to make stepping stones out of stumbling blocks." - Jack Penn

There is no greater elation than achieving something that you once believed to be difficult to attain. Having aspirations to be better in the future than we are now is what keeps us going. I believe we are destined to mimic the universe and constantly expand. It's just a belief I have but I am sure some scientist or philosopher has explored it a lot more deeply than I have. I just feel it in my gut.

Hope is the thing that spurs us on in this eternal quest. Viktor Frankl, in recounting his devastating experience of the Nazi concentration camps, noted that when he saw fellow inmates lose all hope, he could often predict how many days it would be before life left them. He goes on to say that it's beating challenges that is pretty much the point of life.

So, it could be as ordinary a challenge as the Couch to 5k, it could be to tick seven countries off your travel bucket list in the next year, it could be to learn sign language or to build a new social life, or it could even be to have a six figure business or sign a book or recording contract.

Whatever the challenge you set yourself - never forget that it's yours. I strongly recommend telling people if you feel they will be positive and supportive or if you think it will spur you to be accountable or work harder towards your goal. I equally strongly recommend keeping it to yourself if you know, deep down, that those around you are inclined to rain on your parade in the guise of 'bringing you back to earth.'

Whichever you decide, here's a few tips on goal setting.

1.Be realistic. (As a bit of a dreamer, who still believes in fairies, I really dislike this phrase and I would never piss on anyone's bonfire. However, if you are 53 then it's unlikely you are going to be the next England football prodigy and if you are six foot three it might be tricky to achieve that career as a Jockey.)

2.Then, be really bold and venture a bit further. Amanda Frances, the multi-millionaire business coach is a self-proclaimed 'achiever of unrealistic goals' and I love this. (Hence my one million pounds for charity target.) It's not a challenge unless it's a bit of a stretch. There's no point setting yourself Couch to 5k if you are already doing 4k three times a week!

3.Break it down into its smaller parts. There is absolutely no doubt whatsoever in my mind that this helps hugely. If someone told me I had to run 5k with no training then I would baulk. However, if I knew I could stop for ten seconds every 800m then I would see that as do-able.

4.Never beat yourself up if you don't fully make it. Instead, celebrate the wins; I have been teased for starting too many things and not finishing - sometimes by those who could do with being a little more adventurous in their own lives.

I rejoice at all the crazy ventures I have tried. There is no shame in trying. I love the fact that I have set out to be, do and have so many different things in my life and just because not all of them have come to fruition does not make me a failure.

Chapter 18

Face the crap head-on

"Manana is often the busiest day of the week." - Spanish proverb.

There is a lot to be said for facing up to the things we really want to put off - those annoying jobs we just don't feel up to - the awkward conversations we would prefer not to have. There are books, websites, Facebook groups, whole communities devoted to the natural human affliction we call procrastination. I know fellow therapists and coaches who have it as their speciality, with clients who pay them good money to help them overcome it.

If there was a Nobel Prize for it, I would definitely be a contender. In fact, if you are reading this book then that is a miracle in itself as I have started writing at least a dozen different books and even got close to finishing a few of them but, to date, this will be just the third one I have actually completed and published!

So I know that me saying 'just do it' is not going to be enough to get you moving in those areas you are avoiding. What I can do, though, is help you understand what is going on. What I can promise is that on the other side of 'putting it off' is the joy of achievement.

Procrastination is born of fear. No matter how big or small the fear - that is simply what it is.

Usually, in some form or another, it's the fear of not being good enough.

Once you can see or acknowledge the fear, it becomes easier to rationalise; tackling those nasty jobs ahead of everything else soon becomes a whole lot easier.

The weirdest thing about this is that the fear is just as likely to be a fear of success as one of failure.

We are inherently attached to the familiar, to what we know. So if we perceive failure as our 'normal,' the whole idea of success can be pretty terrifying. We like what we know, however negative it might be.

Facing the crap head-on is definitely an ongoing work in progress for me. My mum has always been good at knowing it's best to get the chores out of the way. The only downside of this is that if you tell yourself 'I'll sit down when I've got all my jobs done,' then you may never sit down!

A perfect balance to this could be to intersperse those pockets of productivity and nasty tick-list jobs with little mini treats and breaks.

As students, my best friend and I would always leave our most dreaded assignments until the last minute. (I never listened to Mum in those days.) In other words, we would start the night before it had to be handed in! We'd tell ourselves we 'worked better under pressure.'

So we used to devise little reward systems to ensure the work got done - it involved staying up all night but twenty year olds can handle it.

We would lock some chocolate and a bottle of cheap wine into one of the kitchen cupboards and arrange to meet at midnight for a quick cream egg break then carry on essay-writing. (I think the wine was for when we had finished - probably breakfast time!) Needless to say, it did the trick.

It has taken me many years to appreciate the joy of 'getting it out of the way.'

Chapter 19

Write a letter

"Letter writing is the only device combining solitude with good company." - Lord Byron

Write a letter. Not an email, but a handwritten letter. On paper. With a nice pen. It doesn't really matter who you write to. You could write a letter to your seven-year-old self. Or to your eighty-five year old self. Write to the Prime Minister telling them how to do their job better. Or to the Queen telling her you like her (or not). You could address it to a long-deceased loved one with all the things you wished you had said or asked. Do it with love and a belief that, somehow, they will get the message.

In my childhood, we used to have pen friends. The art of letter writing was seen as a desirable skill. It was exciting to write a letter to someone whose face you could not even picture and even more intriguing to see their unfamiliar penmanship in a reply a few weeks later (yes patience was a thing in those days).

There are plenty of ways that writing a letter can lead to great joy. One is in the act of handwriting itself (see chapter 11 about journaling). Another, it's a brilliant way to spew out feelings - good, bad and ugly - onto a page and therefore out of ourselves; sweet joyous release.

If the outpouring turns out to be more 'word vomit' than 'poetic ode' then remember, you could always let it all go by burning it and allowing the ashes to float off on the breeze under a pale full moon.

Thirdly, my favourite, is the prospect of getting a reply! (For this it must be sent to a real, living person.)

If you decide to write a letter to your inner child, pour out everything you wish someone had told you at that age. Start by praising that little child. We all need praise, love, encouragement and positive vibes. However, not everyone receives this in their childhood. This may or may not be the fault of parents and in many ways it's irrelevant why you may not have received enough praise; you cannot change the past, but you can learn to frame it in such a way that its impact on the here and now is vastly altered in a positive way.

A brilliant way to help with this is to find a photograph of you as a child. Notice the innocence, the openness, the readiness to become a person, a fully grown, full-bloom human being. Send unconditional love in the form of a beautifully crafted, heartfelt handwritten letter.

Chapter 20

Volunteer

"What is the essence of life? To serve others and to do good." - Aristotle

Volunteering, in my view, is not the same thing as doing good deeds. The two may be closely related but volunteering is much more about planning and committing to give of yourself, of your time, of your skills. A good deed can be random, unplanned and may barely inconvenience you. Volunteering is the opposite and so it can be proportionately rewarding.

When I was younger, I'm not proud of the fact that I used to take a superior delight in using the phrase 'do-gooder' to describe how I perceived all volunteer-types.

In my mind, volunteering was something for frumpy, middle-aged women to fill up their endless hours of nothing-better-to-do in between church services and cake baking. It had connotations of interfering in other people's lives, of holier-than-thou, a knowing-what's-best-for-you type of condescension.

In reality, volunteering is just plain noble. And joyful.

My experience of voluntary work is limited to working with homeless people in Bristol where I live. Like everywhere nowadays, we have a worryingly growing problem.

Feeding homeless adults, stripped of not just a roof over their head, but of pretty much all pride and spirit, can be humbling, to say the least. The gratitude and humility, the humanity I encountered, truly put my charmed, blessed life into perspective.

These people were largely grateful, well mannered, kind and not lacking in humour despite lacking in bathing facilities, despite the sometimes biting cold and rain.

I made my teenaged self choke down the humble pie that the experience served me up, not just for the unfortunate souls we were helping, but also on behalf of the wonderful people involved in organising the charity. These were everyday people - just like you and me - and they were regularly giving time, money and energy they barely had to give and not an elasticated skirt or pair of Jesus sandals in sight!

I enjoyed the experience; yes, it made me feel good to help; yes, it made me appreciate, more than I ever had before, the warm bed I went home to that night. There were times when I felt close to tears at the plights I was witnessing. But ultimately, it felt good - just to be able to make a small difference.

I believe we are all destined to help others in some way or another and volunteering can take many forms. As can joy.

Chapter 21

Challenge your beliefs

"You must be ready to burn yourself in your own flame: how could you become new, if you had not first become ashes?" ~ Friedrich Nietzsche

How is challenging your own existing beliefs going to add joy to your world?

Our natural instincts mean we are pre-conditioned to spot danger so we tend to naturally live from a place of fear, despite the fact that there is relatively little danger in our modern world compared to the days of the sabre-toothed tiger. Living in fear is not a pleasant state of being and is particularly bad for our health.

The conditioning we all receive from childhood tends to promote certain types of fear. So for example, if you were poor, then you may develop a mistrust of people who are rich and cultivate a belief that being rich equals being bad. Or perhaps you were led to believe that money is the root of all evil. If you grew up in a war zone then you would likely develop a mistrust of a particular nationality, religion or culture as well as undoubtedly suffering from post-traumatic syndrome.

Once we have preconceived ideas, which were formed in our early years, it's very difficult to change them. So then, as adults, we tend to look out for evidence that backs up our prejudices because we all like to feel that we are right.

However, if we can persuade ourselves to challenge our most deeply held convictions, we are opening ourselves up, not just to new ideas, but to a complete liberation from the chains of the old (often limiting) belief systems.

Remember how I said that we are destined to grow, expand, create and add some kind of value to the world? Well, it's much easier to do this when you are open to all possibilities. I'm not saying you should start thinking that maybe the earth is flat after all. However, if you open up to the idea that some of your ideas could be misguided or born of ignorance - and I mean this in the politest possible way - then the world can often be seen in a new, more positive light.

Just try it - I have already noticed that the people I know who believe in fairies and unicorns are among the most joyful I know!

Chapter 22

Embrace your shadow

"Even a happy life cannot be without a measure of darkness and the word 'happy' would lose its meaning if it were not balanced by sadness." - Karl Jung

This might seem a little controversial in a book of joy, but hear me out. Embrace your shadow - I don't mean the Peter Pan thing or the five o' clock variety either.

I mean your dark side - the bit of you that is negative or depressed, the bit of you that needs this book the most. There is nothing wrong with having a bit of darkness within. After all, without the dark there is no light. Everything in the universe is about balance.

Of course we are going to naturally desire more joy in our lives than shadow. It feels better - it's as simple as that.

Take a look at all the examples of polar opposites in nature - night and day, black and white, hot and cold. Most of these illustrate that the one is simply a lack of its opposite. I genuinely believe that there is no such thing as evil - but sometimes there is a complete absence of good.

It's important not to try to supress or deny a whole aspect of ourselves. Merely being aware that you have a facet that is not perfect, or appealing or beautiful or positive is enough to set you on the path of 'warts and all' self-acceptance and, ultimately, self-love. After all, do you love those dear to you any less for their imperfections?

I am not saying wallow in your dark clouds, feed your black dog, wrap yourself in the clothing of despair, just don't beat yourself up if you have mean thoughts or days where you just hate everyone and everything.

Acknowledge the shadow and move on. Try to celebrate it as an essential backdrop to your brilliant light so that it can shine ever more brightly.

Chapter 23

Emanate love

"Love is our true essence." - Mata Amritanandamayi

Without love, there can be no joy - the two are inextricably connected. If you can develop a habit of infusing love into every situation you encounter, you will find that life becomes an equation of 'input equals output' and love will return to you ten times, a hundred times over - in the form of joy.

When you start to put negative, pre-formed opinions and thoughts aside and start to live life from a place of love, it soon becomes clear that a heart-centred approach to life is the most valid and successful as a way of navigating the world in a joyful way.

Have you ever pondered the often-used phrase 'I just know in my heart of hearts?'

There is a knowing when we use our heart instincts over our head and this is because the thoughts in our brain are processed via the five senses and are designed to protect us from danger by sparking the survival reflex of fear.

Love's polar opposite energy - hate - is fed and fuelled by fear.

So, if we work backwards and start by filling our heart with love, then very soon hate or jealousy, anger, mistrust and any other negative emotions will have no room to exist.

To begin with, it will take effort and you will have to try to fill your heart with love. It will be conscious. However, repeated, conscious action soon becomes natural, unconscious action - it's how all habits are formed.

So close your eyes and take a deep breath in and feel love flowing into your heart centre - imagine a beautiful green spinning vortex where love energy resides (not the physical organ that pumps your blood).

Next, imagine an aura all around you. This aura or energy field is your essence, your being; it's the very flavour of you. Send love to this aura, to the beautiful being that is your mind, your body, your spirit. See it as being much bigger than just the 'you' that you can see in the mirror. Picture it as all-encompassing. Imagine it spreading out and growing to include the whole of the universe - all of infinite space and all of eternal time.

Now amplify that loving feeling and love yourself ten, a hundred, a million times more. Feel the warmth of a universal hug from you to you. Say out loud or in your head: 'I love you.' It's a wondrous thing to do each night before you sleep.

Chapter 24

Use kind inner dialogue

"The most important words you will ever hear are the words you say to yourself." - Marisa Peer

Another joyful and effective daily practice (great for the mornings) is to look in the mirror and send yourself love. It may feel odd at first but it absolutely works. Look deep into your own eyes and say out loud. I AM ENOUGH. Write it on your mirror so that it's there constantly and you see it subconsciously every time you glimpse it. Because you ARE enough. You are perfect in all your perfectly human imperfection.

Once you become comfortable saying this, then try graduating on to the more powerful 'I LOVE YOU. You are lovable.' Because you are lovable and you deserve to be loved. Even if you genuinely feel that the only person in the whole world who truly loves you is you - that is enough validation. In fact, it's the only validation.

The first step to being loved is to love you. It's almost impossible to give or receive love to or from another person until you come to terms with loving yourself. It's never too late to change how you feel about yourself.

Start by changing the words you speak to yourself internally on a daily basis.

Once you start paying attention, you may notice that sometimes you can be harsh on yourself. I recommend comparing it with how you would speak to someone you love dearly - a grandparent or small child is a good place to start as they are often a source of unconditional love. Would you speak to that person in the way you speak to yourself?

Or you could, instead, imagine you are speaking to your inner child - your four year old self. Think about how it would impact them if you berated them daily. When it comes to voicing things out loud, tone of voice is almost more important than what you are saying. Remember, if you infuse your words with love, it's almost impossible to be unkind. When you use kind words and a loving tone of voice your joy will always be nearby.

Chapter 25

Look for beauty

"Never lose an opportunity of seeing anything beautiful, for beauty is God's handwriting." - Ralph Waldo Emerson

Beauty and joy are great friends. There is no doubt that beauty is subjective, it's in the eye of the beholder and this is great news because it means that all around us there are things that are beautiful at least to someone.

Beauty can be found in the simplest of things - from a stunning piece of fine art to an ugly new-born Pug - it's simply a matter of taste.

Here are a few things that I find beautiful: sunset, sunrise, autumn colours, mountains, lakes, trees, forests, beaches, human faces, tigers, lavender fields, starry nights, the moon, birdsong, smiles, babies' voices, classical music, laughter, youth, old age, butterflies, dragonflies, crystals, kindness, dogs, childbirth, the sea, you, me.

Let's take the human face. My own personal idea of a beautiful face is not necessarily the bland, supermodel version of youthful male and female beauty (although I can recognise the perfection of the faces on the covers of magazines) but the wizened face of a third world centenarian who has survived war, disease and famine, or the loving faces of an elderly couple who have been happily married soul mates for sixty years.

One of the most beautiful sights I saw recently was a woman wearing traditional African robes, western trainers on her feet, carrying a huge bundle on her head with grace and poise as she walked down a deserted, suburban English street near my home in Bristol.

When I am too busy to be out there in the world, I indulge in Pinterest as it's the most visually pleasing of all the social media platforms and if you simply type the word beautiful in front of anything from deserts to desserts, from dresses to dressers and all the stars, waterfalls and mountains in between, then you can be sure to find something that pleases your eye.

PART TWO – REST

Synonyms:

Recover

Refresh

Revitalise

Restore

Revive

Relax

Replenish

Repose

Chapter 26

Sleep

"Sleep is the golden chain that ties health and our bodies together." —
Thomas Dekker

In short, sleep is good for us and a lack of good, healthy sleep is
detrimental to our physical and mental health. It's simple science. That is
why sleep deprivation is used as a form of torture and probably why I get
tearful when I am tired. If you struggle with getting good sleep then I
strongly recommend you focus on changing that.

How many joyful insomniacs do you know?

I confess I have not always been the best at sleeping. It's a skill I envy in
others.

Here are a few tips I have used to get better at it. Make your bedroom as
nice as it can possibly be - I have tried to make mine feel like a place of
calm and repose. Wash your bedsheets just a little more often than you
currently do (unless you are already a bit OCD). There is nothing more
luxurious than snuggling under clean sheets.

Pay attention to your sleep hygiene - that means keeping a regular bedtime routine, going to sleep at the same time each night. Try to avoid having devices on, or watching TV/doing anything overstimulating prior to bedtime.

I use sleep meditations - either guided or just lovely music (this makes it impossible to switch off all devices but it works for me.)

If you are light-sensitive, try an eye mask and use earplugs if the slightest little sound keeps you awake.

Other things that are supposed to help are: hot baths, lavender, a banana before bed, malted/milky drinks, and ensuring you are not vitamin deficient - especially magnesium.

Beware also of drinking alcohol to help with sleep - it's merely a clever deception. A few glasses of something before bed may seem to have the effect of helping to knock you out more quickly. However, the overall quality of the sleep you get is worse, due to the fact that, as your liver processes the alcohol, it causes a disruption to the balance of the four important cyclical sleep phases and so you don't get the same quality or overall length of sleep. In addition to this you will wake up feeling dehydrated and groggy.

Chapter 27

Connect with Mother Nature

"I took a walk in the woods and came out taller than the trees." - Henry
David Thoreau

Spend time in nature - soak up the sun, talk to robins and butterflies,
collect shells, leaves, acorns, pebbles.

This is one of my absolute favourite pieces of advice. There is nothing
more soothing, refreshing, invigorating and life-affirming than being out
in nature. You don't have to hike mountains, forests and lakes to enjoy the
beauty of our wonderful planet. A simple walk in the park is enough,
sometimes, to feel connected to nature.

Open up your senses to every aspect of the experience, hear every twitter
of birdsong, notice every beautiful clean crisp blade of grass, see the ever-
changing dissimilitude of each moving cloud in a sky that's never, ever
the same as it was just minutes or seconds before. Just really take in
everything around you and you cannot fail to experience joy. Being out in
nature is a wonderful way to affirm that you are properly alive, fully
present and are a tiny part of a much bigger, universal tapestry. There are

other chapters about the physical, wellbeing aspects of grounding, tree hugging, being around water, but the best starting point is to appreciate the miracle that is the natural world we encounter every day.

If that means nothing more than pondering your own unique irises in the mirror and marvelling at their absolute one-of-a-kindness in a seven billion-populated planet, then that is fine - you are part of Mother Nature.

Have you ever tried to get your head around the fact that the petals of a rose grow in harmony with a perfect geometrical pattern? Or, even more mind blowing, that a mere human called Fibonacci had the mental capacity to discover that remarkable connection between nature and mathematics? Did you know that water can crystallise in different ways according to the type of energy it's exposed to? Positive energy creates organised, uniformed structures and negative gives more chaotic, distorted crystals. How does it know? I'll leave that with you....

Chapter 28

Take a shower

"Go green, be 'eco,' save water, shower with a friend!" Ali Todd

Take a shower. Yes I know it seems obvious doesn't it? But I don't just mean any old shower. I'm talking about really relishing the experience, really loving and enjoying the cleansing nature of the moment. Use this daily routine to tap in to your inspiration and intuition. There are many 'Eureka moments' that I have had in the shower (ha!) and lots of inventors, creatives and innovators credit their morning shower with some of their best ideas.

It could be that this is the only moment of uninterrupted peace you get in your day. So when you take your morning shower, try to imagine a stream of beautiful, silver-bright, heavenly light pouring down through the crown of your head. Picture and feel a wonderful, healing energy and light as it trickles down through your body, cleansing, rebalancing and realigning your chakras. Allow this imagery to energize you and to penetrate your entire being.

Research has shown that switching to cold water towards the end of your shower actually sends your body into healing mode. The slight shock of cold water on your skin is surprisingly good for your immune system. In addition to this, it's invigorating, stimulating and refreshing. It leaves your skin feeling toned and revitalized. If you can stand the breath-taking shock, it will elevate your mood and allow you to start your day feeling fully alive, full of energy and totally awake.

Like singing, having a cold water shock can have a positive impact on the function of the vagus nerve - a bodily system that is being increasingly recognised for its crucial role in our healing and immunity. Definitely not for the faint hearted though!

Chapter 29

Eat well

"Let food be thy medicine and medicine be thy food." - *Hippocrates*

Of course eating well is important for our general health but can it really impact the joy we feel? Well, in my opinion, yes and the reasons are twofold.

Firstly, plenty of research has shown that certain foods can have a positive impact on our mood. We all know that if you are a chocoholic then there is a definite buzz associated with consuming it. But there is a whole list of healthy foods that scientists have found to be mood enhancing.

I was delighted to find, during the course of my research, that, unwittingly, I consume many of these in my morning porridge/granola concoction. They include bananas, nuts, seeds, oats, berries, yoghurt, and coffee. In addition, oily fish was on the list, as were beans, lentils fermented foods containing probiotics and dark chocolate, which I love because it gives a much more instant hit than calorific milk choc and my 'off switch' kicks in sooner.

Secondly, the act of eating is pleasurable - it's meant to be enjoyable so that we don't forget to do it, thus keeping us alive. In addition to plain old survival, in modern society, eating has become a wonderful way to socialise and connect with those around us. Now that most of us no longer have to kill or grow our own food, we have the leisure to try other flavours, tastes and recipes. Food is a brilliant door into cultural exchange and awareness, a wonderful way of celebrating the differences mankind has developed across our glorious planet.

Who hasn't looked forward to a night out at a restaurant with friends, both for the social aspect and for the possibility of exploring new tastes?

Now, more than ever, this is relevant and being able to eat out again is something I am really looking forward to.

So what does 'eating well' look like? The answer to that question will differ according to taste; however, the obvious is moderation, balance, self-control and variety.

This is not a diet book. However, one thing I will advise, as someone who has tried to lose weight for years, is don't go on a diet. They completely kill all joy. Lifestyle changes, even small ones, are far more likely to have a long lasting impact.

One recent trend in eating habits that I cannot resist mentioning is fasting. Although it appears to be a new fad, it has actually been around for years, not least in most religious communities.

There are many definite health benefits of intermittent fasting too numerous to list here. In terms of joy, though, not only does fasting stimulate something called BDNF (Brain-Derived Neurotropic Factor that has an important role in brain function, including mood regulation), indulging in this voluntary discomfort also increases our appreciation of healthy, nutritious food and so has a positive all round impact on our relationship with food.

Chapter 30

Smile

"A smile is the best makeup any girl can wear." - *Marilyn Monroe*

Smile. Whether or not you feel like it. Science has shown that just the placement of facial muscles into a smile, even a fake one, will release happy hormones to your brain in the same way that they would if your smile was spontaneous and real. So the old chestnut 'fake it 'til you make it' is actually true in this instance.

Smiling can literally trick your brain into feeling joy.

Joy is not the only benefit of smiling. Have a look at yourself in the mirror when you're not smiling - maybe, like me, you have a 'resting bitch face' - not a good look. When I was younger, my non smiling face just looked neutral. Now it looks indisputably miserable. I'm not advocating going round with a permanent idiotic grin on your face, but there is no doubt that smiling looks much prettier. And what about laughter lines? Yes, they can be ageing but I prefer to see them as a beautiful, detailed map of a joy-filled life.

Another brilliant thing about a smile is that you can afford to give away as many as you like and it costs nothing. With any luck, someone might just give you theirs in return and getting one from someone else definitely adds to your joy. So next time you are walking down the street try it on a stranger. You may feel shy - sometimes we don't have the courage to actually say hello so a smile is a perfect alternative.

Now, Covid has seen us having to cover up our lower face and I find this devastating. So I have been practising smiling with my eyes over the top of my mask - it's quite an art - one practised for years by women who wear the niqab that leaves only the eyes visible. A smile can be subtle, nuanced and still give you and others joy.

Finally, if nothing else you can see it simply as yoga for the face, stretching the muscles and improving the blood flow, counterbalancing the lines it creates.

Chapter 31

Stretch

"You are only as young as your spine is flexible." - Joseph Pilates

Stretch your body. It does not necessarily even need to be yoga or Pilates. Just the act of stretching and pushing your limbs and muscles to do things outside of their normal day to day boundaries is good for your body.

Challenge your body to be as flexible as it used to be when you were younger. This can be a gradual process whereby you get better and better each day. You don't need to be a fitness instructor to see that stretching is good for your blood circulation, your flexibility, your muscle memory and your overall physical feeling of well-being.

You could even have a goal such as trying to do the splits or touch your toes. Perhaps just doing old-fashioned side bends, twists and lunges is enough. Only you can know your own body but there is no doubt that it's a wonderful feeling when you are able to achieve something today that you couldn't do yesterday and it's surprising how quickly you can see improvements if you make stretching a daily habit.

Of course, yoga is brilliant for stretching but it's a commitment that takes time. There are plenty of online videos that will show you the basics for free. The sun salutation is a fabulous way to start each morning or you could simply devise your own mini stretching routine.

My dog stretches every morning without fail and I trust in his more finely tuned instincts as a good example to follow.

The reason stretching makes us feel good is that it activates the parasympathetic nervous system - this is the part of our nervous system that relates to rest and relaxation and so it induces a feeling of calm and relieves stress.

There is even some research showing that stretching can help to naturally increase our levels of human growth hormone and this has many positive effects on our health and better health equals increased joy.

Chapter 32

Enjoy human touch

"To be able to feel the lightest touch really is a gift"- Christopher Reeve

A very important part of any loving relationship is touch. Now you may not be in a physically intimate relationship with anyone at the moment and that's ok.

Nevertheless research has shown that physical touch is an essential part of human wellbeing. It stems from the fact that as babies we are touched, cuddled and held frequently just by the very nature of not being able to feed, care or fend for ourselves. This imprint stays with us and as a result, all through our lives, physical contact with other humans is representative of being loved, cared for and safe. Even the formal touch of a handshake represents trust. Scientists know that we experience a release of oxytocin, the feel good hormone, as well as raised levels of serotonin, when we experience skin to skin contact and at the same time we see a drop in the stress hormone cortisol.

If you find yourself in a situation where the physical touch of another person is not available to you, is there anything you can do to compensate?

Yes, is the short answer. When you can only meet friends and family online, be sure to give each other a virtual hug - literally hug yourselves on each other's behalf. It may seem weird at first but giving yourself an all-encompassing squeeze will go some way towards replacing the real thing. Plus, if it makes you all feel a bit silly then it's likely to lead to laughter - another brilliant form of free, drug-free medicine.

In addition to this, deliberate self-touch can be very soothing (and I don't mean 'touch' of the naughty variety - that's another chapter!)

Basically, any form of self massage is good for you, whether it's simply slathering on a load of moisturising lotion after a shower or giving yourself a tension-busting head and neck massage. I highly recommend those weird devices with the bendy prongs to give yourself the most delightful, tingly head massage (it won't replace your actual touch - just feels nice).

The key to this is to spoil yourself; to do it with love. There is no one in the world that deserves your love more than YOU!

Chapter 33

Pray like a seven year old

"Any concern too small to be turned into prayer is too small to be made into a burden." - Corrie Ten Bloom

Praying like a seven year old is different to the normal, grown up style of counting our blessings. Practicing daily adult gratitude for all the good things in life is vital for our overall mind-set and definitely has a positive impact on how we view our lives.

In addition to this, every night before you go to sleep say your prayers in a childlike manner. It doesn't matter if you believe in God, or Buddha or Allah - just ask, with blind, unerring faith, for the simple blessing of those you love.

When I was a kid, my sisters and I would go to my grandparents' house and my Nan would always make us say our prayers at night. It always ended up being a long list of God blesses; God bless Mum, God bless Dad, God bless auntie blah blah, and so on. The beauty of doing this in your adult life is that it makes you think about people who are not so close anymore, all those you just don't see very often, but still care about.

It's a brilliant way of expanding beyond the tiny little circle of your daily nearest and dearest. You don't have to include your whole Christmas card list, but it wouldn't do any harm to pick a few people from there just now and then.

One of my favourite hymns when I was a child went something like this; ' thank you for the food we eat, thank you for the world so sweet, thank you for the birds that sing, thank you Lord for everything - Amen.' Could it get any simpler than that? Basically, 'thank you, God.'

So another useful prayer might be to bless your food and give thanks for it. I know it's a rather old-fashioned thing to do to say grace; however, no one needs to know.

It feels joyful to acknowledge and give thanks for these basic gifts in life even if you are totally agnostic about whom or what you are thanking.

Chapter 34

Breathe

"When people ask me what the most important thing is in life, I answer: Just breathe." - Yoko Ono

Breathe. Not in the obvious sense - I'm not talking about the breathing I do without thinking, the breathing that is automatic, dictated by our autonomic nervous system, but the kind of breathing that is conscious: the sort that your yoga teacher encourages you to do. To this end, try becoming aware of your breath, making it a deliberate and calculated action.

A technique recommended by yoga instructors is to breathe into your abdomen picturing your breath traveling down through your energy centres or chakras.

Conscious breathing is very useful for relieving anxiety.

The method that is recommended for coping with panic or anxiety attacks is called square breathing, and is based on the premise that focus on the breath will both distract you mentally from the trigger of the attack at the same time as lessening the physiological impact.

If you breathe in the square pattern, it switches the active nervous system from the fight or flight reflex to the parasympathetic nervous system that promotes calm and rest. You simply imagine a square, breathe in 2,3,4, hold 2,3,4, breathe out 2,3,4, hold 2,3,4, and imagine going round the four sides of the square about ten times.

However, you don't need to be suffering from anxiety to benefit from the many positive advantages of conscious breathing - it simply makes you feel good, it's a brilliant affirmation of life and nothing beats being out in the fresh air and gulping in a nice greedy lungful of the stuff of life.

Chapter 35

Hug a tree

"If you want to have peace on this planet full of stress and turmoil, go to a tree, and hug it." - Banani Ray

The Japanese have long known the benefits of the energy exuded by trees and plants. I have taken a lot of stick (excuse the pun) about it for years but I am actually quite proud to be a tree hugger.

The ancient art of forest bathing - known in Japan as Shinrin Yoku - is now being prescribed in some parts of the world to help people with stress and other ailments.

I know that if I am feeling down and I go out into the woods first thing in the morning it sets me up for the day and I urge you to try it for an instant fix of joy.

Here's how to make the best of it in order to get a massive boost to your vitality:

Leave all digital devices at home or at least switch them off.

Make a conscious effort to actually connect with the natural world around you. Allow your feet to take you wherever they want to go - this is the beauty of going with the flow - there's no need to have any kind of plan.

Tune in with all of your senses for a proper burst of restorative, cleansing tree energy. Notice all the magnificent, beautiful hues of green around you - or in autumn the visual cacophony of fiery colours.

Taste the freshness of the air - the temperature is always a couple of degrees cooler in the woods and this feels like the epitome of outdoors. Breathe in the distinctive smell of fresh air - I relish the earthy, ironey tang it gives my skin - when we were kids and we had been playing outdoors Mum would say we smelt of 'dirt and worms.'

Pay attention to every sound around you - birdsong is simply the most beautiful sound in the world. Allow the breeze to caress your skin.

Don't be afraid to literally hug a tree. I find they are perfectly sized for human arms to go round and when I do it I see it as a sharing experience. I silently thank the tree for sharing its beautiful vibes with me and then in return, I offer some of my own mental images and love in return - often I will picture the ocean as I figure this to be something the tree has never experienced (who can be sure?)

Chapter 36

Ground yourself

"Flying starts from the ground. The more grounded you are, the higher you fly." – J.R. Rim

Grounding yourself is crucial if you want to experience more joy in your life and I speak both physically and metaphorically. Grounding yourself in nature is a wonderful feeling. I mean literally taking off your shoes and going barefoot on the grass or even in the mud. Sand is my favourite feeling - nothing beats the feeling of sand tickling between the toes for a quick burst of joy. If you watch the movie "Grounded' you will see that there are health benefits to be had from the practice of grounding or 'Earthing,' as some people call it.

It has something to do with the charge of the planet as opposed to the charge of our bodies and so we get 'good ions' (my own phrase) from doing this.

If you are uncertain, think about the times when you have felt most relaxed, joyful and at one with life. For me, being on holiday wins, hands down, and I genuinely believe that this is in a large part due to how grounded it makes me. The mix of planting my feet on the earth or beach, paddling or swimming in the sea, feeling the warm or cool breeze on my bare skin and soaking up the scorching sunshine - all four elements Earth, Air, Water and Fire - a heady healing mix.

Camping is a wonderfully grounding experience - not for everyone I admit. Eating outdoors, even in your own garden, has a grounding feeling to it as does sitting around a fire pit, barbecue or camp fire. Climbing Glastonbury Tor and nearly being blown off the top by gale force gusts was the most exhilarating thing ever!

Have you ever watched a kid roll down a hill on the grass? Remember what I said about little ones and their instincts for the outdoors? There must be an inherent reason why they feel drawn to dig in the mud, scrabble in the sand, splash in puddles and play for hours in the rain or snow - basically connecting in the most primal, physical way with the elements. They simply must know something that we don't. Something we have forgotten and would do well to reconnect with.

Chapter 37

Bathe

"There must be quite a few things a hot bath won't cure, but I don't know many of them." - Sylvia Plath

To me, as a bit of an eco nut, a bath is a bit of a luxury, a guilty pleasure. But occasional self-indulgent pampering is a wonderful act of affirmation that 'I am worth it.' Keeping it as a rare treat makes it all the more special and I highly recommend a beautiful, bubbly, candle-lit, scented soak just once in a while for pure feel good factor.

A long, hot bath is a blissful way to relax and has been shown in studies to help reduce tension, stress and anxiety as well as alleviating some symptoms of depression, and can even ease anger and aggression.

It's a great body temperature regulator too; if I get too cold in the winter it's the only thing that can warm me up. I love bathing in Epsom salts or essential oils for soothing aches and pains.

If a morning shower ending with a cold blast is brilliant for stimulating ideas, a warm bath at the end of a long hard day is the perfect way to wind down and relax.

For many of us, locking the bathroom door for a languid soak is the only moment of peace and quiet, of uninterrupted solitude and reflection time available in our busy lives. Having a bath is probably the first mental image I see when anyone mentions having some 'me time.'

The ultimate act of self-care, it's also the perfect aid to deep, replenishing sleep as warmer body temperature promotes synchronisation of our circadian rhythms.

Candle light is the perfect antidote to the constant glare of digital blue light overload. Use scented candles and play some gentle music or nature sounds and nirvana will soon feel just a whisper away.

Bathing in water has been shown to reduce the stress hormone cortisol and can even aid digestion.

Historically, communal bathing has been used to build community and socialise. Maybe that explains the huge rise in our modern day equivalent - the hot tub. Perhaps it's because our skin is our largest organ that there is something so soothing about being submerged in water; chatting with friends at the same time is icing on the cake.

You could even go so far as trying open water swimming - now that would be truly exhilarating - it has all the benefits of being sociable at the same time as giving the body that healing power of the cold shock. Picture those news items where you see a bunch of really old people who are still pretty comfortable doing that crazy Boxing Day swim in icy waters with not a hint of ill health between them. (Take care not to swallow the water if you are in untreated water - Weil's disease is pretty nasty).

Chapter 38

Meditate

"By the practice of meditation, you will find that you are carrying within your heart a portable paradise." - Paramahansa Yogananda

There are a gazillion meditations out there nowadays so take your pick. You can meditate on getting richer, slimmer, calmer, sleeping better, having a kundalini brain rush or exploring the quantum field, the list is endless.

The most important thing to appreciate about meditation is that it's meant to do none of those things and all of those things.

Most importantly meditation is about connecting with your best self, your higher self if you like. It's about connecting with peace, with the divine within.

So for this reason, my favourite type of meditation for Joy is heart centred. The aim is to fill your whole self up with love - what could be more joyful than that?

There are whole books on the subject of meditation but here is a quick suggestion of how you might want to start.

Get comfortable - it's not compulsory to sit like an ancient Buddha or expert yogi.

Allow your breathing to slow into slightly deeper breaths than normal - breaths that are evenly timed (about four seconds in four seconds out).

If you can keep your breathing evenly timed it's a brilliant shortcut to feeling steady and relaxed. Switching all thought off is far from easy but if you repeatedly return your focus to the breath then you are half way there.

I recommend listening to some kind of guided meditation to start with - you will find that once you get more familiar with what to do, you will manage by yourself.

Some popular apps include Calm and Headspace but there are plenty of freebies to be found on YouTube as well.

It's up to you whether you use music or prefer silence.

Beyond the meditation, I recommend just trying to find brief moments throughout the day when you can tune into an elevated feeling of calm, love and peace. It's often during the busiest most chaotic times that we most need these snatched minutes to zone out and tune in to joy.

Chapter 39

Do nothing

"Beware the barrenness of a busy life' - Unknown

It seems like this could be the same as mediating but I can assure you it's not. When I meditate, I am consciously tuning into an awareness that my busy brain normally blocks me from accessing. There is bliss in meditation.

Doing nothing is no less of a skill, and it can also be blissful. I suppose the most obvious block to achieving joy through doing literally nothing is guilt. In Western, capitalist society, we are trained from a young age to believe that hard work is the only virtue, that we should be constantly trying to 'achieve' and so idleness is seen as sinful, bad. Yet, visit a farming village in any developing country where surely they work harder than is comprehensible to many of us and you will see villagers squatting in groups, watching the world go by, passing the time of day with each other, spending joyful, guilt-free, purposeless time in each other's company doing nothing. Maybe we need to learn a lesson from this. Not every minute of our time needs to be timetabled.

Chapter 40

Practise gratitude

"Wear gratitude like a cloak and it will feed every corner of your life." -
Rumi

There is a reason why we say 'practise' gratitude - it's something you can get better and better at. It's literally an on-tap source of joy that we can tune into whenever we want or need to.

It's something that everyone can do - you don't need to be on the Forbes rich list either. You only have to look at the smiling faces of dirt poor African villagers, Indian street people, Latin American slum kids to realise that in the absence of all else, the air we breathe and the life force running through our veins is a gift to be grateful for.

I have found that the more I remember to notice all the things I have to be grateful for, the more things I find to notice. For example, yesterday I watched a film about a young man who suffered from permanent hearing loss. It made me really think about how grateful I am for my hearing and this led me to feel immense gratitude for all my senses.

It's quite inspiring to write these things down in a gratitude journal because then you can go back and look at things you have felt grateful for in the past. The practice of feeling gratitude definitely cultivates joy and it's a brilliant counterbalance to any vision board or wish list you may have. Focus on what you do have and more good things will come. As my wonderful grandparents used to say: 'Count your blessings every day.'

Chapter 41

Reminisce

"It is never too late to have a happy childhood" - Berkeley Breathed

If you do this with the right intention then it is a wonderful, on-tap, giver of joy. It is a treat to be savoured and, like chocolate, not to be overindulged for the danger of living too much in the past.

Just occasionally I love to treat myself to reminiscences of the happiest moments of my childhood; the Christmases, family holidays, paddling pool days and moments of family hilarity at silly things like farting, playing snap in the caravan while the rain beat down; doing Frank Spencer impressions and teasing our poor mum - the butt of almost every family joke.

Nothing gives me a warmer feeling inside than remembering the gentle kindness and old fashioned humour of my grandparents and their totally unconditional love.

I give myself the giggles reliving crazy girl's nights out in my twenties and thirties, although I definitely don't miss the hangovers.

Most of all, I get a surge of joyful, heart-filling love energy when I reminisce about my now independent, adult children when they were just adorable toddlers who were all mine and I was their entire world.

Whether or not you had a happy childhood, or have your own family, we all have moments of happiness from our past to draw on when we need to. Sometimes it's just a matter of placing your focus on the simple bits. Like the excitement when you realised that muffled morning silence almost definitely meant snow. Or that time you were certain you heard Santa's sleigh bells over the roof. Perhaps it was the joy of your child's first steps or the comfort you felt to hold your dad's huge hand when you were still so small. Do you remember that smell of the year's first grass cut, signalling lighter, longer, easier days to come? Or the excitement in the pit of your tummy at the prospect of delightful summer holidays stretching endlessly ahead?

Reminiscing is an art worth honing and one I recommend sharing with others.

Chapter 42

Drink water

"Water is the driving force of all nature" - *Leonardo Da Vinci*

Most people know that the human body is made up of around seventy percent water, but did you know that the brain consists of even more at around eighty percent?

It's common knowledge that keeping hydrated is vital for our overall health and that lack of hydration can lead to fatigue, brain fog and even overeating because some of us find it hard to distinguish between true hunger and thirst.

However, what is less publicised is that lack of hydration can lead to lower mood as well. This is because one of the roles of water in brain function is to detoxify and cleanse so that it can function as it should and one of these functions is to keep all our mood hormones in balance. In addition to serving the brain, getting plenty of water helps with heart function as well as every other system in our amazing human bodies.

For me on a more personal level, because I am not a natural drinker of adequate water, just knowing that I am drinking enough feels like an instant win and that gives me joy on a psychological level before the physical benefits can even kick in.

In addition to this, I have had to get creative because my natural sweet tooth makes me want to add unhealthy concentrates with artificial sweeteners. Instead, I have experimented with using iced herbal, spiced and fruit teas and infusions. Some of the best spices for mood enhancement, according to research, are ginger, cardamom, cinnamon, turmeric and ginseng. Mint leaves, raspberries or cucumber also all make water taste better.

Chapter 43

Soak up the sun

"Turn your face to the sun and the shadows fall behind you" - Maori proverb

I think the sun gets a bad press these days, yet it's common knowledge that the rays from the sun are good for us, both physically and psychologically. Sunshine causes our bodies to produce essential vitamin D - a key part of our immune system.

Unfortunately, in recent years, skin cancer warnings have eclipsed the fact that humans are becoming alarmingly deficient in this immune-boosting vitamin.

As with everything, balance is the key. I know on an intuitive level that being in the sun puts me in a good mood and so I seek it out whenever I can (whilst remaining mindful of being sensible with its powerful but healing rays).

Having a bit of a tan makes me look and feel better, younger, healthier and brighter. Although it's very important to avoid burning, I believe it's equally wise not to burden our largest, most sensitive organ with too many paraben-loaded sun creams. Ultimately, it's a simple matter of common sense.

It's believed that in order to get enough vitamin D, around fifteen to twenty minutes a day spent outdoors with exposed forearms will suffice but of course this will vary from person to person and depends on factors like skin tone, cloud cover, time of day and what part of the world you live in.

I was nevertheless surprised when I realised how easy it should be to top up our levels of this vitamin - surely most of us can manage that? Even in this land of rain and cloud! Hmm, then again... As a precaution, I take a supplement in the winter with Vitamin D in it.

It's not all about keeping a healthy immune system though. For me, the joy-inducing effects of the sun are far more instantaneous. I find it impossible to be miserable when the sun is out and I definitely feel lower in the winter months when sunlight is a rarer treat in my country.

There is a good reason why the sun has been worshipped for thousands of years as an all-powerful symbol of joy and giver of all life. Think about the connotations of the word sun and its link to joy - she was a ray of sunshine, he has a sunny disposition, she thought the sun shone out of his backside, finding your place in the sun, to have your moment in the sun, to be a sun worshipper. I find it hard not to be!

Chapter 44

Laugh

"Everybody laughs in the same language because laughter is a universal connection." - Yakov Smirnoff

Laugh. In addition to smiling, another wonderful way to feel joy is to laugh. Laughter is famously the best medicine. When we laugh, we also release dopamine, endorphins and other happy hormones into our brain. There's nothing better than a good laugh, especially the kind where you almost end up in tears. The best way to do this is to have fun with friends and family. What's your favourite comedian? Mine's Mickey Flanagan.

There's even a case for forced laughter. I went to a Laughter Yoga workshop in Bristol years ago with the brilliant, wacky Joe Hoare. It was really weird - almost like a drama class. It started with warm up exercises, just walking around the room, starting to relax and so on and then it progressed to using your voice a bit like humming etc. then finally, you were encouraged to laugh out loud. To literally force yourself to laugh. It was embarrassing and I really thought "I can't do this." But before too long it just got easier and the very act of laughing, forcedly, started to make me laugh. The very fact of being in the same room with a bunch of strangers taking part in exactly the same nutty exercise soon turned my pretend laughing into genuine unfettered laughter. Try it - there's probably something online if you don't happen to have a class nearby.

Alternatively, you could join an online laughter yoga group.

Worst case, just look in the mirror, force yourself to laugh, sustain it as long as you can and before you know it, it becomes real unforced, joyful laughter. Remember not to worry about those laughter lines because they are a sign of joy, and therefore attractive, appealing human and real.

Chapter 45

Create a sanctuary

"I've learned that home isn't a place, it's a feeling." – *Cecelia Ahearn*

Your sanctuary does not necessarily have to be your home, but if that is where you love to be then it's a good start. The definition of a sanctuary, for me, is somewhere where you feel safe and at peace; a place you gravitate to when you need to retreat from the stresses of daily life. For the most part, my home is my sanctuary and I suspect this is the case for most of us who are blessed enough to have one.

I also take sanctuary in the imaginary world of fiction novels; I take sanctuary in the music I love; mostly, I take sanctuary in the company of my partner, my kids, loved ones and family. Other times they can be the very thing I am seeking sanctuary from! It can be a movable feast. It could be that you take sanctuary in your hobby or that it can be found simply in the soapy bubbles of a hot, candle-lit bath with a 'Do Not Disturb' sign on the door.

The key thing is to know where that place is for you and to take yourself there, guilt-free, whenever you need to. The guilt-free bit is crucial. We need sanctuary in our lives in order that we may function to the fullest capacity in all that we do. To rest and escape in the most complete sense is a right not a luxury, especially if, in any way, your life involves putting others first.

No one can give from an empty cup and no one can serve others with joy when they are knackered. 'Running on empty' is a very apt description of what it's like to run out of joy. It's quite a simple thing. Where or what is your sanctuary? Go and refill your joy.

Chapter 46

Practise patience

"Patience attracts happiness; it brings near that which is far." - Swahili proverb

Several times now, I have mentioned self-restraint or even voluntary discomfort in order to increase joy. So fasting, cold showers and gardening have all been shown to lead to joy. Those things are not exactly the first that come to mind when the word joy is mentioned. So how does it work?

Well, for me it's about appreciation. Here's an example. We recently went camping and the weather was rubbish. I love camping but hate being cold. Even though I enjoyed myself, it was only on returning home to a centrally heated house with hot shower and warm cosy bedding that I was able to really value what I have. Likewise, when I've been unwell, I often don't realise how bad I was feeling until I begin to feel better.

Negative comparison can really boost good feelings. I suppose it's just another way of counting our blessings - imagining what life would be like without even the simplest of luxuries, such as running water, can be a powerful gratitude trigger.

And patience? I believe that waiting for good things can have the same effect. Perhaps it's no coincidence that we live in an era where gratification is more instant than ever before and yet the incidence of depression and poor mental health is at its highest.

Maybe it's because we have lost the virtue that is patience. They say 'all good things come to those who wait' and patience is actually used as a measure of emotional intelligence in children. There was a well-documented study where a group of children were offered the choice of either one sweet right now or two sweets if they waited until later on.

I genuinely believe that if we can learn the art of self-imposed delayed gratification then the 'good things' we wait for will be all the sweeter.

So I urge you to try it in some form - I'm not suggesting you take up bird watching or learn tantric sex (although there's no harm in slowing it down a bit). Maybe just resisting the 'box set binge' in favour of good old fashioned weekly episodes, or setting the 'wine o' clock' hand back an hour will suffice. Waiting patiently for strawberries to be in season will surely mean tastier, juicier fruit than any bland, cold-stored import?

It's about finding the things that give you so much joy that they are worth waiting for - then waiting patiently, safe in the knowledge that whatever it is will be all the more joyful for the wait.

Chapter 47

Forgive

"Forgiveness is the fragrance that the violet sheds on the heel that has crushed it." - Mark Twain

To forgive is sometimes the hardest thing in the world to do. Yet, it's a crucial rung on the ladder to joy.

It seems hard to comprehend how, when an inflicted pain is drastic, the sufferer is still able to forgive. It's hard to make sense of stories where a mother can forgive the murderer of her child yet *I* find it hard to forgive an ex for cheating on me eons ago!

Perhaps the vain sting of hurt pride is more falsely blinding than the raw, agony of true heartbreak. The former is more about the ego and less about the soul.

There is a universal truth that forgiveness often serves the victim even more than it serves the wrong-doer. In forgiving, you free yourself from the shackles of resentment, anger, hatred and this liberation releases us to feel joy once more.

There is no pretending with forgiveness; it has to come from the heart. Forgiveness can never be a counterfeit currency.

Nevertheless, I believe it's something you can achieve with continued practice and effort. Not that there are degrees of forgiveness - you either forgive or you don't. But if you keep trying it on for size, eventually it will fit. You, alone, can know when you have reached the point of forgiveness; it's easy to tell because your heart will be relieved of its heavy burden. A grudge relinquished is like a prison door smashed open, releasing you into joy.

The most powerful form of forgiveness is forgiving yourself. We tend to be far harsher with our own failings and misdemeanours than we are with the wrongs others do to us.

A good place to start when trying to forgive others is to ask yourself the following question and then try to answer it honestly: was the pain caused intentionally? Most people do not set out to hurt others, they more often do it by default, a by-product of a selfish action rather than a pure evil intent.

On the other hand, if you are convinced that someone deliberately acted to cause you pain, then the best way forward is surely forgiveness anyhow? Because, in forgiving, you take back the power into your own hands. As Oscar Wilde said; "Always forgive your enemies; nothing annoys them so much."

PART THREE - PLAY

Definition: 'A physical or mental leisure activity that is undertaken purely for enjoyment or amusement and has no other objective.'

Chapter 48

Spend time around children

"Adults are just outdated children" - Dr Seuss

Spend time with small children. As a former teacher I'm completely biased about this one and I have yet to find many things that give me more joy.

I just love the sound of children playing and, of all the joyful moments this rewarding profession can offer, there was nothing I loved more than watching the children play freely at playtime. I could spend all day watching them, wondering what thoughts and ideas were going through their mind as they played creatively in pursuit of crazy, unfathomable missions of the imagination. For me it was vastly entertaining.

Even those of you who don't think you like children can benefit from the golden energy that kids emit. Watch them play, listen to them sing and watch them dance.

My favourite scientific study about this was the BBC TV series where they brought a group of pre-schoolers into an elderly people's care home to spend time with the residents. The positive impact on so many aspects of their health and wellbeing was noticeable, measurable.

By the end of the series, all the metrics regarding the elderly people's cognitive and physical function were measurably improved - even to the point of giving one or two residents a renewed desire to carry on living - a desire that they had previously been very close to giving up on.

It was also lovely to see how well the children took to the old people too - and at times amusing - just as cats always seem to gravitate to those who are allergic to them. I remember one adorable child taking a real shine to one of the grumpier residents who had never really had any contact with kids and completely winning him round!

Small children don't judge and this is priceless. They have no reason to assume anyone will not like them. They know they are lovable. If only we could all keep that part of ourselves.

Not all of us are lucky enough to work in a school or have children or grandchildren of our own but even if you don't know any small children, there are plenty of ways around the situation - just be careful about randomly approaching mums in the park and asking if you can borrow their kids!

It might be possible for you to volunteer in a school; they are always crying out for volunteers to hear kids read and there are organizations who hook 'reading buddies' up with a suitable school. (Subject to screening checks.)

Another gem I discovered is a TV show called The Secret Life of Four Year Olds. It's a genuine, fly-on-the-wall, peek at the world of little ones and how they interact. For me it's pure, undiluted joy and, often, comedy gold.

An even quicker shortcut to joy is the sound of babies or toddlers laughing and giggling. There isn't a more beautiful, joyful sound in the whole world

- I've known people have it as the ringtone on their phone. I defy even the most hard-hearted, joyless among you to try this and not find benefit.

Have you ever looked, really looked, at a very young baby? Try it. I urge you to try looking beyond the scrunched up wrinkly face and see its soul. I believe that when we look into the eyes of a brand new life, we are able to see a tiny glimmer, a reflection and memory of who we were when we were born.

Because we are all a pure, untarnished blank canvas at birth. We are all made up of pure love and so, when you look deep into the eyes of a baby, it can feel like you are staring into the vast mystery of the universe itself.

Chapter 49

Spend time around old people

"I'm not getting old. I'm evolving." - *Keith Richards*

To celebrate getting older is to celebrate life. Every day is a gift. Every wrinkle, a mark of still being here. Even those age-related ailments are (according to my doctor) 'better than the alternative.'

I love reading about initiatives to bring young and old people together because I know that therein lies a chance to forge meaningful, loving and mutually beneficial friendships.

If you are still young then it may be hard for you to see any appeal in the idea of spending time around old people. I know that when I was young, I often saw them as grumpy, judgemental and just plain boring.

What I have learned now that I am in my fifties (an age I consider to be 'in between') is that the key to getting the best out of old people, in fact any people, is to ask them about their lives. Be interested in them. Listen to what they have to say. No matter how humble their achievement in life, it was old people who built the world you and I were born into. They paved our way. Whether or not you believe they did a great job, there are many ways in which their struggle was significantly harder than our lives today.

So for that reason alone, show them the respect and appreciation they deserve and you will bask in the reflected glow of their happy memories. It helps to ask the right questions. It helps if you are genuinely interested in what the world was like in their youth. Most of us love to tell our story. It won't take long to realise that, not only can they remember what it felt like to be young; they still feel exactly the same on the inside! You won't get that from reading a history book.

Most of all, take heed of any lessons they try to impart; they (I feel like I should be saying 'we') have the advantage of experience and when they come out with clichés about how quickly time flies and only getting one shot at life or to make the most of every minute, remember that clichés evolve because they are true!

Chapter 50

Create things

"You can't use up creativity. The more you use, the more you have." - *Maya Angelou*

Create something. The human species is designed to create - we are natural creators and it's a fundamental drive in our existence. So we procreate, we also create via our thoughts, actions and emotions.

From the simple act of cooking a meal to the most complex feats of engineering and everything between, mankind is destined to expand and grow, to improve and construct our world, to breathe life into the imagination of our ever-growing existence.

One of the most common self-criticisms that people make is that they are not creative. Everyone is creative; anyone who gets up in the morning and decides what clothes to wear, what breakfast to eat and what activities to pursue on any given day, is creative. You don't have to be Picasso or Mozart to create.

The beauty of creativity is that in most cases, it allows you to get out of your head and into a meditative state where a part of your soul is connected to the source of all creation.

As a starting point you may choose to purchase a simple colouring-in book, or have a go at learning a tune on the recorder or a rhythm on a drum. (Just remember there are only so many times your loved ones will tolerate hearing the same tune.) Perhaps you want to crochet or knit or sew. Even reading fiction requires adequate creativity to imagine the manufactured world of the story.

An exercise I do often with children I teach in order to show them that they do have creative ability is to describe a basic scene to them. They love the fact that when I go back and ask them to fill in the details, everyone has different versions of the same scenario.

I'm sure all the readers among us had slightly different images in our mind's eye of just what Harry Potter may have looked like until the silver screen turned him into Daniel Radcliffe.

Creativity can take a million different forms. You may put on make-up in the morning; you may decide how the barber should cut your hair. If you have ever planned an event such as a birthday or wedding party then you have used creativity.

What is important is recognising this and accepting it in order to expand it and do more of it.

Chapter 51

Wear different clothes (play dress up)

"Fashion should be a form of escapism and not a form of imprisonment."
- Alexander McQueen

Wear something different - use your clothes as a way of having fun, of stepping outside of your comfort zone. This idea is twofold; it embodies both creativity and the stimulus of breaking old, boring habits.

During lockdown, I tended to wear the same old dull, boring outfits that were based more on comfort than aesthetic appearance. It became too easy to just tell myself that there was no point in dressing up with nowhere to go.

However, on the occasions where I forced myself to change this habit, I felt noticeably better about myself and my life in general. I highly recommend playing around with colour - for too many years of my life I was a 'black is slimming' person (long after I unknowingly became a 'black is ageing' person).

What a waste of the beautiful gift that we humans are blessed with - that of being to enjoy the beauty of colour. It sets us apart from the animals and is a vital part of our creativity. They say that dogs see in black and white - well, unlucky dogs.

Unlike dogs, we humans are driven to create and perhaps that is one of the reasons we have this wonderful ability to see colour and to appreciate its beauty. It's fun learning what colours suit you; it's joyful discovering something to wear that you would never have entertained in the past and if you are lucky enough to be over a certain age, it's quite liberating to be unrestrained by the limiting bonds of what is fashionable!

Try it. Play around with your wardrobe. Play dress up as though you were a child. Be brave enough to wear a hat. Wear jewellery even if you are going nowhere. Or a biker jacket. (There is no such thing as mutton dressed as lamb if you carry it with boldness and confidence.)

You don't need to be as outrageous as Baddie Winkle (find her on Instagram) unless you want to. Just be you - with a bit more YOU thrown in. Feel the joy.

Chapter 52

Get naked

"And I said to my body softly 'I want to be your friend.' I took a long breath and replied 'I have been waiting my whole life for this'" - Nayjirah Waheed

Now you have had fun with clothes, here's the daring bit. Get naked. I'm deadly serious. Set all judgement aside for a few short minutes and just strip off - preferably in the comfort of your own home/bedroom. Now, be bold and look, really look at what you see.

Ignore the lumps and bumps, skip over the bits you have spent many years learning to hate and simply see yourself. You are not your body, you are not your face, your lines, your weight or you colouring. You are not your grey hair or uneven boobs. You are so much more.

When we are born, we have no judgement of ourselves. We know on some level that we are all created from a universal energy that can best be described as love (if you are averse to the word 'God') so we intrinsically know that we are lovable and loved. It's only the harsh external experience of living that beats this out of us.

We have to take the time out now and then to remember. We ARE lovable. YOU are lovable. In all your nakedness, in your 'birth-day' suit you are lovable and perfect and beautifully imperfect. In short you are unique. Being naked is a wonderful way to come to terms with yourself.

Standing naked in front of a mirror is a wonderful and crazy way of experiencing joy. Celebrate and rejoice at being alive. At being you. At being unique. At being whole. At being one with the source that created you.

We are all special and at the same time, we are all tiny specks of nothing in a vast and infinite universe - a drop in an endless ocean. And if the worst comes to the worst, just have a damned good laugh at yourself!

Chapter 53

Seek a thrill

"Do one thing every day that scares you." - *Eleanor Roosevelt*

There are aspects of this particular way of pursuing joy that are childlike. Think climbing frames, roller coasters and horror films. Yet, even as adults many of us continue to seek the buzz and thrill of doing something that takes us scarily outside of our comfort zone.

Behind this propensity to danger that some of us embrace more than others are some valuable attitudes and traits. The unique experiences we chase can cultivate JOY, fulfilment and coveted memories. New adventures can provide us with the opportunity to grow and expand our sense of self.

You don't need to be an adrenaline junkie to want to get a thrill. By definition a thrill seeker is simply someone who goes after novel, varied, intense and exotic experiences and is not deterred by the risk or danger attached to them.

It's not the actual risk or danger that is appealing; those are mere side effects worth tolerating. So the thrill could be something as simple as joining a sports team, running a marathon or climbing the nearest summit.

I am not a danger person and roller coasters give me migraines but I still know deep down that some of my most joyous, exhilarating experiences have been those where I have stepped right outside of my comfort zone and scared myself a little.

So, yes, zip-wiring was a thrill (obviously) and skiing some of the more challenging slopes is too, but also so was snorkelling in Barbados with turtles because I am not the strongest swimmer and usually hate going under water.

Even singing karaoke sober or driving a car on the right hand side for the first time in Europe have given me the thrill of 'Yesss!! I did it!!' In research, those defined as thrill seekers reported lower stress levels and more positive emotions around self-esteem and happiness.

Chapter 54

Sing

"If I cannot fly, let me sing." - Stephen Sondheim

Singing is without doubt one of the easiest, cheapest, most universally accessible mood boosters we have. Even if you are not a brilliant singer, it doesn't matter. The endorphins released when you belt out a song will be no less potent just because you are no Pavarotti.

One of the mood-boosting hormones released when you sing is oxytocin - otherwise known as the cuddle hormone because it's released by the brain when we have physical contact.

So if snuggling up with a loved one is not available to you right now then having a good sing is a possible substitute.

In addition to the direct joy-stimulating chemicals, there is a wealth of other benefits to our health from singing. They include support in cognition and memory, longevity, and immunity.

There is some evidence to say that singing can stimulate the vagus nerve which is becoming increasingly recognised as a key player in many aspects of keeping our numerous bodily systems healthy.

If you feel too inhibited to sing at the top of your lungs then humming or chanting will come in a close second instead.

Chapter 55

Dance

"Dance is the hidden language of the soul." - Martha Graham

Dance. Dancing is one of the most joyful ways of being in your body. It sounds obvious. I mean, how can you not be in your body? But you'd be surprised how many of us live in our heads nowadays. It's easy to sit for a whole day in front of a screen barely moving. We could be almost robots, just a brain detached from our physicality.

I have always found dancing to be a most joyful thing to do, a release, a way of letting my hair down, really getting out of my head, so to speak.

When you really think about dancing, it's actually the most oddly, bizarrely, strange thing to do. Yet, it's a fundamental human instinct, a basic, primal age-old form of self-expression.

Dancing can be fun; it can be serious, meditational, trancey, hypnotic and plain silly fun. For a while I was a Chakradance™ facilitator. This basically involves talking people through a moving, guided, dancing meditation where each piece of music and spoken word is geared towards helping the participants clear their chakras or energy centres. It was so enjoyable and liberating that I actually wanted to be the participant more than the class facilitator. It epitomised the idea of dance in all its rawness - there were no rules and everyone was encouraged to close their eyes and look inwards. In short it was safe to dance like no one was watching because no one was.

So, I defy you to dance like no one's watching and not feel joy. Even if you end up feeling silly, self-conscious and embarrassed, who cares? If you end up laughing at yourself, so much the better - that kills two birds with one stone.

I highly recommend putting on some music on a Saturday night with your loved ones and having a disco. We have sober discos nowadays and we are getting better at losing our inhibitions without needing booze. I still haven't made it to a silent disco yet but it's on my list. I know it will be fun.

The best thing about dancing is that you need music and music as we all know, is the food of love.

Chapter 56

Play board games

"I think it's wrong that only one company makes the game Monopoly."
Steven Wright

There are reasons why board games are good for us. Like all manner of play, they are like a practice or mirror for real life. When children play, it's a way of rehearsing for life as a human adult. Many of the skills and attributes needed for board games are brilliant for this - turn taking, analysing, lateral thinking, strategy and planning, give and take, winning and losing, honesty, competitiveness, honour, the list is endless.

Talk to many a family on Christmas or other family festivities and they will undoubtedly agree that board games bring out the child in even the most mature among us and not always in a good way.

The reason I recommend it as a means to joy is that it enables you to exercise all those mental muscles I have just mentioned but in a non-pressured way. It all goes back to the human connection aspect that is vital to feeling joy on a regular, sustained basis.

You may sometimes feel like you are losing at life so if you are whiz at scrabble then how joyful to beat your high-powered executive brother? And what a great reminder for all the big shots out there that they cannot be winners all the time.

Board games seem to have made a comeback recently in pubs and bars - probably because they are a great way of having fun with friends without getting hammered.

Puzzles are another relaxing pastime that seems to be on trend as I write. I am looking forward to getting into this as a healthier (mentally) option to all the dark crime dramas that now dominate the small screen and no longer offer me the chilled escapism I crave.

I know I will love it because just over a year ago, I got stuck into a couple of wonderful puzzles at the kid's after school club where I worked. I knew I was hooked when I became so engrossed in completing a scene from Disney's Frozen that it took me twenty minutes to notice that all the 'littlies' I had started the puzzle with had moved on to other play, leaving me determinedly finishing the thing by myself!

Chapter 57

Listen to/play music

"Music is the divine way to tell beautiful, poetic things to the heart." - *Pablo Casals*

Listen to music. There's no better way of getting in touch with your inner self and feeling joy than by listening to music. Other than smell, I would say music is the most evocative memory-inducing and nostalgic sensory experience humans can have.

I love music so much that I cannot concentrate on anything else when there's any playing even if it's on quietly in the background. Especially if there are lyrics. So when I'm working I choose classical music. Ironically, this was something I hated when I was younger. Perhaps it's only us oldies who crave the peace that classical music offers because nowadays, I find it soothing, relaxing and joyful. I am quite choosy and pretty inexpert so I generally pick well-known tunes from adverts and movies.

My favourite way of listening to music is to go and see live bands. There's nothing more fun than a good outdoor festival or gig concert. This surely has to do with the buzz and vibe of crowd energy. There is nothing more invigorating than thousands of people all bouncing in time to the same tune.

I also believe it has something to do with the imperfections and natural, organic feel of music being performed live. You could be in the tiny Zed Alley - one of Bristol's smallest music venues - hearing the first ever live performance of the latest up and coming band's first release. Or you could be at Glastonbury hearing the Rolling Stones' five thousandth live rendition of 'Satisfaction.' Either way you are hearing something unique, something that is so 'in the moment' that it can never be replicated exactly.

When it comes to playing music, sadly I am not a musician. I foolishly rebuffed all my dad's pressure to learn an instrument as a kid, using the logic that I got teased enough already for being a swot and that carrying a violin case to school would only further my misery.

Now, I wish he had insisted! I am bitterly jealous of any friends who can play an instrument even at the most basic level and listening to people I know personally play a tune on an instrument often moves me to tears or at least spine tingles at the very beauty of being able to make music.

For my birthday this year, I got a steel tongue drum - the go-to, de rigueur instrument for any closet hippie like me. I have discovered that anyone can make music but not many of us can make beautiful music!

Chapter 58

Spend time with animals

"Animals are such agreeable friends—they ask no questions, they pass no criticisms." — George Eliot

Spend time around animals. If you don't have your own pet, then it may be useful to visit borrowmydoggy.com. Or ask a neighbour if you can walk their dog. Cats are particularly beneficial because they are low maintenance and still very soothing to stroke and pet.

Even if you don't like pets, then watch nature programs instead. The beauty and miracle of the living world is hard to deny. David Attenborough has a lot to be thanked for because he has bought the vast, glorious wonder of the natural world into our living rooms.

There is nothing more joyful than the playfulness of a baby elephant, the cheekiness of a baby chimp, the resourcefulness of a hungry lioness to really understand what the living world is all about.

Try watching the March of the Penguins for a lesson in unwavering survival, determination in the face of adversity. Or My Octopus Teacher for lessons in the sheer intelligence of adaptability. Check out any of the

Blue Planet series, Jane Goodall chimp documentaries or the moving, controversial Blackfish and I dare you to not to feel some joyful affinity with the planet's wonderful and diverse animal kingdom.

Chapter 59

Spin around

"I've kept alive my childlike innocence. I don't let anything or anyone dampen my zest for life. Now, that's very important." - Mumtaz

Spin around. Another joyful trick stolen from childhood is to just spin your body around. In adults it boosts energy and activates aspects of the endocrine system. Some even claim that this can stimulate the hormones that help with weight loss. This was discovered in some research into the whirling dervishes of Turkey and the Middle East. Through their goal of attaining a spiritual connection with God and the universe, scientists discovered that they were also stimulating the two major aspects of the brain's autonomic nervous system simultaneously - the flight/fight bit at the same time as the 'calming' bit and this resulted in a side effect of feeling bliss and wellbeing.

Try it, at first it feels strange and even a bit uncomfortable. Be sure not to make yourself sick. It can be weirdly satisfying, rejuvenating and most of all, fun. Remember doing this when you were a kid? Despite knowing it might end up making you feel a bit queasy, it was still hard to resist the appeal of this playful childish trick.

There is a developmental reason why children love the crazy dizziness of the roundabout in the playground. It helps with the development of muscle memory and coordination. Plus there is something unique about that euphoric, slightly queasy feeling when you finally stand still but the world keeps spinning.

Even as a young teenager I remember disco dancing in the lounge with my sisters - it was the perfect excuse to spin around.

Chapter 60

Have an orgasm

"Sex is a celebration - of love, of joy, of connection, of having a body, of being animal and of being something more - of being human." - Ali Todd

I did warn you a tiny part of this book would be stating the obvious! If you are easily offended/embarrassed then just feel free to skip this short section - I won't mind.

There is a good reason why this is a separate chapter and not simply included in the one about touch - an orgasm can take place without the touch of another human being. Yes - masturbation is still a taboo subject but so are depression and many other mental health issues. And in my opinion, none of them should be.

Remember, this book is about JOY and it would not be complete without mention of one of the most glaringly obvious sources of human euphoria.

Sorry to harp on about science again but it just keeps insisting on backing me up. Having an orgasm releases the happy hormones that can help reduce stress, anxiety and even pain. It can help induce better sleep, lower blood pressure and can even boost the immune system.

It's not surprising to learn that having a sexual experience with another person gives even more physiological and emotional benefits and, when that other human is a long term, loving partner, the benefits are even greater due to the release of oxytocin, the pair-bonding hormone.

However, that is not always available and given that one of the main drives behind me writing this in the first place was the high incidence of loneliness in our society, I think that 'going solo' needs a mention in the context of sexual gratification/orgasm. Plus there is some oxytocin to be had from self pleasure too.

So if you are on your own/not in a relationship (or even if you are) just do it. It feels good, harms no one (it does NOT make you go blind) and no one need ever know!

By the way - in my research I was interested but not surprised to learn that over-use of porn can hijack the brain's neural wiring and mess with the dopamine/reward process in the same way that abuse of any other addictive substance does. So in this instance, the use of our imagination is yet again a more healthy and appropriate pathway to joy.

Chapter 61

Pay a compliment

"A compliment is something like a kiss through a veil." - Victor Hugo

Pay a compliment. I love this one because it's so easy to do. It's free; it's easy, it makes you feel as good as it makes the other person feel. This is an exercise I often used to do when teaching personal, social, moral and health education lessons. Each child would be asked to pay a compliment to one of the other children.

The beauty of this was that often with younger age groups, the compliments would be very basic and simple. They would say things like 'you're nice' or 'I like your shoes' because these are the simple compliments that we learn from an early age.

Invariably we would try to encourage children to go deeper and attempt to find a compliment that was more profound and meaningful. So we would focus on personal qualities like 'you're kind' or you make me laugh or you're a good friend. You see how simple this can be?

A compliment is a compliment. So even if you tell someone they look glowing today, it can have a profound effect on how they feel and also on how you feel.

Probably the most important lesson to take from this is learning to accept compliments when they are paid to you. For many of us it's even harder to do this than it is to find nice things to say about other people. For some reason, probably because we don't feel good enough, most of us struggle to simply say thank you graciously, then smile and enjoy the moment. A simple compliment can have a long standing impact.

A few years ago, my partner was out walking with his two youngest children, exploring a nature reserve. Out of nowhere, a lady came up to him and simply said, "You are such a lovely dad to your children." What she could not have possibly have known was that he had recently gone through a difficult divorce. He adores his kids and was at a point in his life where he was questioning himself, not just as a father but as a person - divorce really can leave you feeling like a failure. Those few kind words, probably no big deal to that lady, meant a HUGE amount to him he has never forgotten it.

So if you think something nice about someone just tell them!

Chapter 62

Spend time with family

"Family is not an important thing. It is everything." Michael J Fox

This one is so obvious to me that I barely know where to start, except to say that if you are lucky enough to have a family that you actually like then you hardly need me to tell you this one.

I feel incredibly fortunate that if I had the option to actually choose my family, I would still pick them all, exactly as they are.

No one knows you like your family. No one loves you in the way that they do. It's impossible to 'unshare' those common experiences that have made you a family, just as it's not easy to recreate that unique intimacy we call 'family' with someone else.

Nevertheless, family can take many different forms. The only important thing to remember is that you know who they are. I am not referring to blood being thicker than water as I am not even sure if that is the actual reason that the family bond is what it is.

To me family *is* joy.

Chapter 63

Overcome a fear

"There is no illusion greater than fear" - Lao Tzu.

Feel the fear and do it anyway. It really is as simple as that - there's no need to read a whole book with this title (unless you really want to) because the message is simple. Just do it!

Most hypnotherapists know that the two best ways to conquer fears and phobias are to reframe them or to simply confront them. To experience the thing you're afraid of and to come out of it the other side and realise that you have survived is a wonderful, joyful feeling. And it's actually true that what doesn't kill you makes you stronger.

I am not suggesting you go out picking up rattlesnakes or tarantulas but I am suggesting that if you are afraid of public speaking then you should deliberately commit to giving a talk in front of people. Or that you book that holiday destination you have always wanted to go to but have been too afraid to fly to.

Facing and defeating fear is exhilarating and liberating - savour the elation and joy - bottle it if you can because we all have fears in life. They are usually irrational and if we can remember the feeling it gives us to defeat a limiting belief of any kind then it can be used time and time again to rinse and repeat until we are fearless.

Of course, there is nothing wrong with baby steps - if you can learn to pet a Chihuahua, then you can learn to pet a Rottweiler. If you can overcome a fear of injections then you can learn to give blood. If you can overcome a fear of flying then you can tackle the world's greatest zip wire (great fun).

Fear is just an emotion and we create all our emotions - it's just a matter of scaling them up or down. In no way do I intend to sound glib in encouraging you to conquer your fears and phobias and I am fully aware of how debilitating they can be.

If all else fails, then (third and final shameless plug) my Rapid Transformation Therapy is a fantastic treatment for such issues.

Chapter 64

Go on a date with yourself

"Serious art is born from serious play." - Julia Cameron

Go on a date with yourself. Julia Cameron advocates this in her book, The Artist's Way. However, you do not have to be an artist or any kind of creative to benefit from this exercise.

It does not have to mean going to a restaurant and eating a candle-lit meal alone. It simply means treating yourself to an excursion of some kind. Possibly a day out or a cultural visit somewhere that you have always wanted to go.

Simply spend time in your own company. Even if you are alone a lot of the time, being out on a trip to actively experience something by yourself is a different thing altogether. Taking yourself on this type of 'date' is a special kind of treat.

Whether or not you consider yourself to be creative in any way, it's particularly stimulating to creatively solving problems or gain a fresh new look at things, or simply to escape the mundane, day-to-day life for a few hours. It might be something as simple as going to a favourite gift or jewellery shop, visiting a gallery or historic site - whatever floats your boat for a few hours of indulgence or browsing. You don't even need to buy yourself anything. Maybe a visit to a museum is your thing.

When my children were small I used to promise myself that once they had flown the coop, I would revisit the museums, the Zoo, and other historic sites I'd taken them to, only this time I would really take my time to enjoy them. I would read, at my leisure, all the information on the placards with no little pitter patter of impatient feet to distract me.

It could be as simple as driving around an area of your city that you don't know, looking at the houses, walking through a park you've never been to, or visiting tourist attractions on your own doorstep that you've always ignored in favour of traveling further afield. Most cities have perfect hidden gems that even the locals don't know about.

Summary

Of all the pearls of wisdom I've given you here - some my own and plenty borrowed from wiser souls than me - the best piece of advice I can squish into one tiny nutshell is this. Banish fear. Simply say 'NO' to that nasty little piece of work.

I don't just mean the sort of fear in Chapter 63. I'm talking about the deep-rooted, hidden fears and insecurities that hold us back from being our best selves and from achieving all the dreams and all the joy in life that you truly deserve. Tell that fear to get on its rickety, worthless old bike and 'do one.'

Then, instead, deliberately welcome joy. Say 'YES!' to heartfelt, unbridled joy in your life. It's a choice. It's an action. Go out and look for it. Find it in every nook and cranny. It's there, trust me, and it desperately wants to be a permanent part of your life.

Acknowledgement

I would like to say a huge thank-you to my wonderful family - to Mum and Dad and my sisters who have always shown me so much love, laughter and joy.

Thank you to my wonderful grown up kids who have been a source of such huge joy, mostly through having survived their teenage years! You have all taught me so much and I know I am incredibly fortunate.

To my wonderful man, Dave. For me, you are the true embodiment of the phrase third time lucky! I am so glad I wished you into my life. I am so grateful for the joy and laughter you bring into every single day of my life. Thank you. X

About The Author

Ali Todd

Ali Todd is a writer, therapist and teacher. She is mother to two wonderful adults - a son, Ryan and daughter, Zoe. Ali lives in Bristol with a Cairn Terrier called Buzz and her third, and final, Dave.

References

All the self-help books I have read (or at least the ones that I can remember)

You are the Placebo - Dr Joe Dispenza
The Biology of Belief - Dr Bruce Lipton
The Secret - Rhonda Byrne
The Artist's Way - Julia Cameron
Big Magic - Elizabeth Gilbert
Think and Grow Rich - Napoleon Hill
Autobiography of a Yogi - Paramahansa Yogananda
The Science of getting Rich - Wallace Wattles
Rich as F*ck - Amanda Frances
The Game of Life and How to Play It - Florence Scovel-Shinn
Becoming Supernatural - Dr Joe Dispenza
Get Selfish - Joanna Hunter
Man's Search for Meaning - Victor Frankl
Untamed - Glennon Doyle
Money Is Love - Barbara Wilder
The Miracle Morning - Hal Elrod
The Five Love Languages - Gary Chapman
The Choice - Edith Eger
The Unexpected Joy of Being Sober - Catherine Gray
The Diary of a Young Girl - Anne Frank
The Raikov Effect
I Am Enough - Marisa Peer
The Tattooist of Auschwitz - Heather Morris
The Art of Being Brilliant - Andy Cope & Andy Whittaker
Wild - A Journey From Lost to Found - Cheryl Strayed
The Salt Path - Raynor Winn

Dying to Be Me - Anita Moorjani

The Alchemist - Paulo Coelho

The Wheels of Life - Anodea Judith

The Chimp Paradox - Prof. Steve Peters

E2 - Pam Grout

18 Rules of Happiness - Karl Moore

The Art of Happiness - The Dalai Lama

59 Seconds - Richard Weissman

Anything about or by Carl Jung

Change Your Thoughts, Change Your Life - Wayne Dyer

The Love Poems of Rumi - Rumi

The Power of Your Subconscious Mind - Joseph Murphy

The Power of Now - Eckhart Tolle

A New Earth - Eckhart Tolle

The Seven Spiritual Laws of Success - Deepak Chopra

Feel the Fear and Do It Anyway - Susan Jeffers

Awakening the laughing Buddha Within -Joe Hoare/Barefoot Doc

The Midnight Library - Matt Haig

The Silva Method - Jose Silva - read by Vishen Lakhiani

Afterword

Before you go, I would be so grateful if you could do one thing for me. No, two. Well, three actually…

Firstly, if you enjoyed this book, please remember to give The Simple Gift of Joy to two people you love who would also enjoy it. Maybe they would like the journal to write in too? Here is the link again. https://thesimplegiftofjoy.com

Secondly, I would be very appreciative of an honest review on Amazon

Finally, don't forget to sign up for my newsletter. I can't wait to let you know not if but when we have raised a million for the mental health charity MIND.

Sign up here on my website: https://thesimplegiftofjoy.com

or join my facebook group for more about JOY www.facebook.com/groups/154066853358739

Do you know any kids? Hot on the heels of this little pocket rocket is my 'Simple Gift of Joy for Kids,' so you may want to hear about the launch date as well as any of my fiction novels that are in the pipeline for the future.

Printed in Great Britain
by Amazon